MBA FIELD STUDIES

A Guide for Students and Faculty

Edited by E. Raymond Corey

Harvard Business School Publishing Division
Boston, Massachusetts

94 93 92 91 90   5 4 3 2 1

Library of Congress Cataloging-in-Publication Data
MBA field studies: a guide for students and faculty/edited by
E. Raymond Corey.
   p. cm.
   Includes bibliographical references.
   ISBN 0-87584-251-8
1. Management—Field work. 2. Business—Field work.
3. Business—Research—Methodology. I. Corey, E. Raymond.
   HD30.4.M38 1990
   650'.0723-dc20   90-37157
                        CIP

Contents

Foreword

*F*ield studies courses, offered widely in business schools in the United
States and abroad, provide a unique educational opportunity quite different from the classroom experience. Typically, field studies projects involve a three- to six-person student team working with a faculty supervisor on problems of corporate or nonprofit clients. The central issues may
fall in such broad areas as business strategy, organization structure and
control systems, and work relationships and processes. Or the purpose
of a study may be to develop market information or to study a business
opportunity and make plans for launching a new venture. Project success depends on accurate problem definition, intensive fact gathering
through field interviews and from library sources, clear written and oral
presentation, and effective team management. Thus, most student field
studies teams employ the same skills as professional consulting and task
force teams.

In taking on complex projects, students are often at a disadvantage because they have had little prior experience or instruction in field research
methods and techniques. This book is intended to help. It deals with a
wide range of relevant topics—problem definition, field interviewing, client relationships, team management, working with faculty advisers,
using library resources and survey questionnaires for fact gathering, and
preparing and delivering the written report and the oral presentation.
By understanding "the territory" at the outset, students may be able to
move more quickly into their projects, plan their work more efficiently,
and make a greater contribution. Most of all, they may gain more from
this unique learning experience.

Faculty supervisors as well can benefit from working with project
teams. They may gain a greater understanding of the complexities of

management issues and practices in their fields of interest. In addition, student-conducted field studies projects often contribute to faculty research. Finally, working with project teams may come close to the ideal teaching experience—tutoring small groups of highly committed students in explorations of common interest. In such a context the faculty supervisor serves as team counselor, teacher, and, ultimately, judge.

The final chapter in this book describes these three roles and provides guidance on how faculty supervisors may be effective in each. In particular, this chapter considers the role of the faculty supervisor as evaluator—how to think about the complex task of providing feedback to students.

This final chapter is addressed to faculty supervisors; the preceding chapters are addressed primarily to students. Having students understand the faculty perspective will help significantly in forming and developing the faculty-team relationship. Each such relationship is based on an understanding—a contract—that is seldom written down but mutually recognized. The quality of the faculty-project team relationship is critical to the successful outcome of the project. The better all parties can recognize and deal with the "terms of the contract," the better the educational outcome.

This book has been prepared by members of the Harvard Business School faculty and staff, each writing about his or her area of expertise, with the purpose of making field studies an enriching and productive learning experience. We hope the book is helpful to field studies project teams and their faculty supervisors. If so, we would appreciate hearing about your experiences. In particular, however, we'd like to know where the book falls short in meeting its purpose and to have your ideas about what may be needed to make it more useful to you.

E. Raymond Corey

Project Management

*F*ield studies projects combine characteristics of both management consulting and project management. *Management consulting* is the transfer of expertise so that the client organization will be more effective after the consultant's departure. The expertise may be in problem solving, process improvement, strategic planning, evaluation, and/or client learning. In any case, the consulting goal is a better-functioning organization.

Project management grows out of a different tradition—managing defense and construction projects. It is product- or systems-oriented. The goal of the typical project manager is to get the job done—on time, within budget, according to specifications. The project is a goal-oriented, coordinated effort of limited duration and is unique—unlikely to occur again in the same fashion.

Although consulting is often an individual activity, projects are done by teams and require all of the usual management functions—planning, organizing, controlling, and leading. A project team, however, unlike the traditional bureaucratic organization, is designed to be flexible and rapidly responsive to changes both within and outside the team.

A successful field study depends upon effective project management by the team. By combining the consulting approach with project management skills, the field studies team can achieve both goals—to leave behind a better-functioning organization and to complete the project on time, within budget, and according to specs.

The most important goal of all—and the reason for undertaking a field studies project in the first place—is for project team members to

Note: This chapter was prepared by Professor E. Raymond Corey, George P. Hollenbeck, and Cynthia Ingols, Harvard Business School.

gain a first-class learning experience to complement and extend class-room learning. The field project becomes a laboratory for applying ideas, tools, and concepts to real-world problems. It is an exercise in managing task-focused relationships among team members, client managers, and the faculty supervisor. It gives students a chance to define issues, gather relevant data from a variety of sources, do insightful analysis, and develop creative solutions. Finally, it provides opportunities to learn about a company, an industry, and/or a field of management that is of long-term interest to the members of the project team.

This guide is intended to help student teams deal effectively with the challenges of doing consulting-type work and to enhance the learning experience—and the psychological rewards—for each team member.

We begin this first chapter with ideas for building relationships among team members and between the team and its faculty supervisor. Later sections of the chapter consider client relationships, contract negotiations, and data collection methods.

Chapter 2 takes up written and oral reports. Chapters 3 through 5 consider data sources and collection methods: field interviews, library research, and survey questionnaires. Chapter 6 provides faculty supervisors with suggestions for counseling, teaching, and grading student teams.

The first two chapters pertain to all field studies projects, while the relevance for any one project of the chapters on data collection will depend on the research design. The information, then, on data sources and data gathering techniques is included here for your use as needed.

Building Team Relationships

- *Spend a lot of time together in the beginning to learn each member's skills and agenda. You'll be able to manage the study better later.*
- *One member initially took on the role of leader; however, he tried to push all his work onto another team member and then took that person's slides to incorporate into his part of the presentation.*
- *We each have different styles, approaches, and standards. Our different perspectives on the project led to varying work loads.*
- *One member did a bit more (the other two feel a little guilty).*
- *Communication turned out to be the most important thing: communication with faculty, communication with the client, communication with other team members.*
- *Define the project well—be specific—explore the subject in depth; get team members committed to the whole project, not an individual section. We achieved that and had no problems with "turf."*

As these comments from second-year MBA students suggest, trust is the critical ingredient in strong working relationships, and communication is the path to trust. Of course, some anxiety is natural when any new team comes together. Even though most of the members of field studies teams usually know each other and have chosen to work together, they are not exempt from the concerns of the members of any newly formed team:

- How will I fit in? Will I be able to contribute as much as I would like? Will others recognize my contributions?
- What is the nature of the project? Will it be useful and interesting?
- Will the field study help my career? What about grades?
- Will there be an equitable distribution of work? Will everyone carry his or her share of the load?

These concerns are typical. Recognize that everyone is a little anxious and provide plenty of time for getting to know each other and discussing these concerns. Time and effort invested in team building will pay off in managing conflict successfully and overcoming some of the inevitable barriers to teamwork. These barriers include:

- different personal goals, priorities, and interests
- unclear project objectives
- disagreements or uncertainty over roles
- a dynamic project environment
- competition over team leadership
- personality clashes
- different work styles

Most of these barriers can be overcome; all can be recognized and managed. For most teams some conflict is inevitable; it usually occurs when expectations are violated. Whenever one person's behavior runs counter to the expectations of another, anger and frustration usually result. It is therefore important to set forth clear expectations and to discuss a process for dealing with unexpected problems as the project proceeds.

Here are some conflict management methods:

- **Withdrawing**: simply withdrawing from the fray may be effective for minor concerns or intractable issues that don't seriously affect the project. The danger is that the problem will worsen rather than diminish.
- **Smoothing**: *de*-emphasizing differences and *re*-emphasizing areas of agreement can place the conflict in perspective and enable the team to move ahead.
- **Compromising**: seeking a solution that meets everyone's needs, at least in part, may be useful if the project goals are not undermined.

However, when an optimal solution or a "right answer" is essential, a compromise may not be the best method of resolving the conflict.

- **Forcing**: mandating one solution or point of view at the expense of others is usually a last resort, inevitably resulting in a win/lose climate.
- **Confronting**: getting team members to confront issues, identify optional solutions, and make decisions as problems arise is often the most effective way of dealing with conflict.

A simple, effective tactic is the start-stop-continue exercise. In the team-building session, each person lists what he or she wishes the others in the team would start doing, stop doing, and continue doing. At their most constructive, these lists describe behaviors that can be changed (e.g., X often misses team meetings for recruitment trips; Y is always late with reports). If feedback can be focused on specific behaviors that slow or frustrate the team, then lags in productivity may be reversed.

Planning and Organizing

- *The work load was divided according to personal constraints and skills. Given the team structure, it worked out to the satisfaction of all sides.*
- *Recommendation: establish not just one overall task plan but several sequential two-week plans and hold every individual to equal burdens (equal in overall context).*
- *People have different priorities and work habits.*
- *Our initial division of work ended up with some assignments being more intellectually demanding and others more routine.*
- *Start early; form a team with complementary skills and abilities; arrange financing as soon as possible and set firm milestones to which all team members must adhere.*
- *Plan and submit a schedule for the study—it helps to manage time at all stages with all people; come prepared to interviews. Write down everything and retype everything. Three months is long enough to forget but too short to repeat interviews.*
- *Preparation and follow-up are time consuming, but worth every second.*

How to begin? As a first step, set aside a block of time to determine goals, processes, and project organization. Consider the following questions:

- What is the core task? How do we do it?
- Where do we want to be in weeks 2, 4, 6, etc.?
- What do I expect of others on the team in terms of commitment, contribution, and work relationships? What does the team want from me?

- How should decisions be made (consensus, majority, or subgroup assigned to tasks)? Who makes what kinds of decisions?
- How do we organize?

Field studies teams will usually emerge from the "getting started" phase with a statement setting forth the project and its goals, start and end dates, a budget, and project milestones. Now begins the detailed planning and organizing of the work.

Successful field studies teams have found that planning is absolutely critical to success. Finding the right balance between defining the project gradually and doing the detailed planning is an important early decision. Close off the project definition too soon, and detailed planning turns out to be a waste. Postponing planning results in costly delays in starting on the data collection.

A work breakdown structure (WBS) is the most important part of planning. Teams will find their own formats; some variant of PERT/CPM is often useful. The WBS lists the major tasks required to complete the project, how they are interrelated, who is responsible for each, the resources needed, and the information flow requirements. As a rule, the more complex the project the more critical formal planning becomes.

Here is a simple example of the first part of a WBS for a hypothetical project:

Work Breakdown Schedule for Software Team[1]

Project: To develop a plan for introducing ABC software.

Responsibility: Team start: December 1, 1989

End: May 5, 1990

Cost: $10,000

Task 1.0 Familiarize Team with ABC

Task 1.1 Review ABC Manual and tryout on PCs

Responsibility: Team

Complete: December 15

Cost: $0

Task 1.2 Visit company and review with engineers

Responsibility: Toni and Sue

Complete: January 1

Cost: $500

---

1. Reprinted by permission from Harold Kerzner and Hans J. Thamhain, *Project Management for Small and Medium Size Businesses.* © 1984 Van Nostrand Reinhold, Inc.

Task 1.3 Report to team on product strengths and weaknesses
> Responsibility: Joe
> Complete: January 7
> Cost: $0

Task 2.0 Review Competitive Products
> Responsibility: Ann
> Dates: January 1-January 31
> Cost: $1,500

In addition to serving as a key planning document, the detailed work plan becomes the basis for monitoring progress. Without an agreed-upon plan containing an appropriate level of detail, progress cannot be charted and variances identified. Regular team meetings give all members an opportunity to review project status and to replan, reallocate resources, and reconsider budget needs if necessary.

Flexibility is important. The focus of the project may change at the request of the faculty supervisor, of client managers as you interview them and collect data, at your own initiative as you get more information, or in response to changes in the company or industry. Expect change; be flexible, but still plan in detail.

Organizing the work involves assigning the tasks to be accomplished and establishing coordinating mechanisms. Because the field studies project is an educational experience, efficiency should not be the only criterion for dividing tasks. One team may spread the work so that all members have as much exposure to as many areas as possible; another may assign work based on member expertise.

Field studies teams report that everything takes longer than expected. And Murphy's Law is known to prevail in project management. Thus, teams often recommend front-loading the work—plan to do as much of the work as soon as possible, leaving a buffer at the end, rather than vice versa. The extra time at the end may make the difference between an orderly completion and having to "pull an all-nighter."

The basic coordinating mechanism is the team meeting; it is the key to managing your field study. Team meetings can be used to brief one another, to keep everyone on board, to refine the problem definition based on new data, to share leads on data sources, and to reinforce team member commitment to the project's success. As the project progresses, new tasks will arise, and the team meetings can be used to assign the tasks and to monitor expenses against budget.

Project complexity will, of course, determine how much communication is required. Weekly meetings may be sufficient. (One team reported telephone calls among members nearly every day.) The rule is,

overcommunicate. Meet frequently; spend a lot of time together inten-
tionally, not merely in response to unanticipated crises.

Who is responsible for managing the project? Unlike a typical industrial or military project team, the field studies team usually starts without a designated project leader. The team as a whole is responsible; how
management responsibility is allocated will vary by team. It is important, however, that team members understand and agree on how the
management functions will be accomplished. Some teams appoint a
project manager; in others, individual team members take responsibility
for different parts. Some teams appoint a coordinator, and others let the
role evolve. Informal leadership often emerges based on contribution to
or interest in the project. Difficulties arise when a team member assumes
the leadership role without consensus.

Working with the Faculty Supervisor

Think of the supervisor as a consultant's consultant. His or her perspectives on procedure, project scope and objectives, knowledge of available resources, adequacy and relevance of data, methods of analysis, and
knowledge of the client can be of great help to the team. Faculty supervisors will evaluate and monitor progress. Don't expect—or encourage—
them to do your work—that is, to plan the project, decide on work methods, analyze data, get directly involved with the client, or make
recommendations.

Your satisfaction with your field study experience will hinge significantly on developing an effective working relationship with your faculty
supervisor. As soon as you can, find out his or her ideas about:

- the end product: written report, oral report, or both?
- frequency of meetings
- content of meetings
- criteria for project success and grading
- assigning grades: the same grade for all team members or individual grades? If the latter, how determined?
- scheduling the final oral presentation for the client: location and
  date

In some instances, as one team reported, faculty supervisors have become too involved:

> The biggest problem we encountered was that our adviser adopted too
> much of a "hands-on" approach, which was detrimental to our group's
> productivity. Even though we were told that we were in the "driver's
> seat," we were not. We wasted a great deal of time trying to determine
> what our adviser wanted and then trying to accomplish it. What he
> wanted was often contrary to what we thought was the best approach

*to the project. Not only was time wasted, but our self-confidence was
diminished by his feedback and, more importantly, the manner in
which it was delivered.*

An early meeting between the team and the supervisor should explore
both the team's and the supervisor's expectations. This is not a time to
gloss over differences or uncertainties. Contracting with the faculty supervisor is part of the process. Without clear expectations on both sides,
unproductive conflict is likely to occur during the project.

Although faculty supervisors have typically worked with several field
study teams, each team and each project is different. If you find your
needs are not being met or you have conflicts with the supervisor, don't
hesitate to deal with those conflicts constructively through frank and
open discussion.

Preparing a Project Proposal

Field studies projects are of two types: (1) those generated by faculty
members and included in a menu of projects for selection, and (2) student-initiated studies. The latter category includes consulting-type projects for business clients, new venture feasibility and planning studies,
and topical research in a field of student interest, e.g., movie film distribution in the United States.

The first step in a student-initiated project is to prepare a proposal for
the approval of a prospective faculty supervisor. If approved, the proposal becomes the contract between the project team and its supervisor.
Its purposes are to qualify the project for academic credit, to establish its
feasibility, to define its objectives, and to outline a project plan.

As for the substance of the proposal, one field studies course description suggests the following:

1. A 2-3 page executive summary and general description of the
   project, including its major objectives.
2. The questions the field study is designed to answer.
3. The analysis you intend to do to help answer these questions.
4. A list of the data required for this analysis.
5. Where you expect to obtain this data from.
6. The proposed plan of action and detailed schedule of the project
   (activities and dates), including milestones for intermediate work
   products that we will review.
7. A description of the team organization and the roles team members
   will play.
8. A working outline of the final report that will be produced.

9. A summary of the resource requirements of the project and how they will be met.

10. Any special confidentiality requirements and how these will be handled.

11. The résumés of students who will participate in the project.

Field studies course heads in other areas may specify some variation of this proposal outline.

Project proposals are not required for faculty-generated field studies. In some cases, however, the faculty supervisor may ask that the student team submit a more definitive and detailed project statement following the initial meetings with the client.

Working with the Client: Mapping the Territory

The first meeting with managers in the client organization typically has a lengthy agenda. Thus, in planning for the contracting meeting, find out how much time the client is scheduling for it, who will be there, and any particular topics the client will want to be sure to cover.

Project team members should go into the meeting with a description of the company and the particular business unit, a preliminary statement of issues, and the name of the contact person. In addition, it's useful to do some library research to obtain any publicly available information on the company and its industry.

You should have a clear understanding of what each team member hopes to gain from the project, e.g., an opportunity to learn about a company and/or industry that may be of career interest; practice in designing and managing team projects; a chance to address a socially significant issue. Having a clear sense of what you want is essential in working with client managers to structure the issues, identify sources of information relevant for the project and for your own learning, develop the client relationship, and negotiate for access to those in the sponsoring organization who can be of greatest help to you.

Obviously, it is essential to have a clear understanding, too, of what the client hopes will come out of working with you in a consulting relationship. Client expectations should be discussed explicitly in the first meeting—and again as team members get to know managers in the client organization. Among the many possibilities on the client's agenda are these:

- **Market information,** e.g., Who are the buyers? How do they buy? What is our image among users and/or resellers of our product? How large is the market and what is its rate of growth? How do we rank with our competitors on after-sale service?

- **Problem resolution**, e.g., interfunctional conflicts; inordinate time lags in new product development processes; excessive work-in-process inventory build-ups; a new product failure.
- **Strategy formulation**, e.g., business unit, product marketing, financial, or manufacturing strategies.
- **Organizational structure and processes**, e.g., an appraisal of the control system, the marketing organization, the R&D/manufacturing interface.
- **Organizational development**, e.g., bringing managers up to date on accounting and control methods, forecasting, or the design and use of information systems; enabling managers themselves to deal with problem resolution and/or organizational change.
- **Evaluation**, e.g., assessing the efficacy of the purchasing function, evaluating the field service operation, appraising the quality of distributor relations.
- **Mediation**, e.g., working with managers in different organizational units to resolve conflicts of interest or differences in strategic objectives.

Another matter to be discussed in the initial client/team meeting is the perceived urgency of the work to the client. When must it be completed? How critical is it to the organization? The greater the urgency, the more likely the client managers will be to make themselves accessible and to comply with requests for data. It is, of course, also more likely that the work will be given high priority at top management levels. Furthermore, the greater the urgency, the more likely it is that the project will culminate in the organization's taking action. A sense among team members that the client perceives the project as an academic exercise should lead to concerns about its ultimate success.

Identifying the Players

The issues cannot be defined and the client commitment assessed, however, until the project team is sure that it understands who the client really is. To whom in the organization will the team address its report? Who will be responsible for accepting or rejecting the team's recommendations and taking action? If a faculty supervisor has developed the project lead, with whom did he or she deal in the client organization? Was that person acting on his or her own behalf or as an agent for someone at a higher level of management? One outcome of the first client/team meeting, then, is either to have confirmation of your initial understanding regarding client identity or to flag some uncertainties on this matter. If uncertainties remain, any confusion should be brought immediately to the attention of the faculty supervisor, and the team should ask for his or her help in clarifying the roles of the several players in the client organization.

In addition, it is important to identify, as soon as possible, those persons in the client firm who are useful sources of information and opinion, those who may be contacted for obtaining source documents and/or arranging meetings and making hotel reservations, and that person to whom expense accounts are to be submitted for reimbursement.

Building Trust

Perhaps the most critical task of all in an initial meeting—and one on which project success hinges—is to begin to establish trust on both sides. Personal concerns such as the following may at first outweigh the client manager's desire to tackle the important business issues.

- Can I trust these guys with what I'd like to tell them?
- What don't I want them to know?
- This wasn't my idea, but will it help me in my job?
- Can I keep this exercise under control?
- Do I want to talk to these students at all?

A client manager's needs for reassurance—clearly part of the hidden agenda—may be satisfied, at least in part, in several ways. First, demonstrate some understanding of the company and the industry and, perhaps in conversation, try to relate this knowledge to other industries and companies that you may have studied in the MBA classroom. Second, share the manager's concerns about the importance of the problem, showing that you understand it and recognize its unique aspects. Third, you might discuss the manager's involvement with the issue at hand as well as his or her role in the firm or department. These can be "low-key" exchanges. They may serve better to build trust than attempting to establish team members' qualifications through a display of MBA-acquired knowledge and business buzzwords.

Once the client manager is comfortable with the project and those who will carry it out, he or she usually becomes less concerned about personal risks and more willing to share knowledge and ideas. Not often do managers have the opportunity to converse with an interested outsider about the nature of their jobs, the lessons of experience, and their perspectives on how problems happen and how they can be resolved! Perhaps, then, the best way to establish trust is to be a good and understanding listener.

Members of the project team, in turn, may have their own concerns about trust:

- Are these people really committed to seeing this through? Will they cooperate in giving us the information we need and making key people available?

- If learning about this kind of business is important to us, will we be able to tap into their knowledge and expertise at a high enough level to make it worthwhile?
- Will they want to use us in ways we don't want to be used?

Team members have the greatest negotiating power in their first meeting with client managers. Tactfully but firmly, then, team members should be forthright in raising questions of commitment and cooperation and should look for explicit answers. In particular, they should be sure that they understand and "buy into" the client's concept of the purpose of the project. If, for example, it turns out that what the client really has in mind is industrial espionage, the project is not legitimate from the students' perspective.

Peter Block, a professional consultant, sums up the agenda for the first meeting as follows:

> What's important to remember here is that you only undermine your leverage if you underplay your own needs and wants at the beginning. . . . The business of the contracting phase is to negotiate wants, cope with mixed motivation, surface concerns about exposure and loss of control. . . .

In the course of the meeting, you should be able to:

- Ask direct questions about who the client is and who the less visible parties to the contract are.
- Elicit the client's expectations of you.
- Clearly and simply state what you want from the client.
- Say no or postpone a project that in your judgment has less than a 50/50 chance of success.
- Probe for the client's underlying concerns about losing control.
- Probe for the client's underlying concerns about exposure and vulnerability.
- Give verbal support to the client.[2]

Negotiating the Contract

If at all possible, given time and travel constraints, the negotiation of a definitive contract is best saved for at least a second meeting, after you

---

2.   Peter Block, *Flawless Consulting* (San Diego: University Associates, Inc., 1981), p. 45. Reprinted by permission.

and the client have gotten to know each other and after you have had a chance to talk among yourselves about the first meeting. The contract doesn't have to be in writing (unless required by your faculty supervisor), but it would certainly be helpful if you and the client had a file memo of what you agreed on. A written summary is useful for later reference, for possible renegotiation, and, at the very least, as the source of an opening statement in your final report.

The contract should be explicit about:

- who the client is—the person or persons who will negotiate the project objectives, to whom the report will be addressed, and who will have responsibility for taking action
- issues to be addressed
- what you won't cover
- the product to be delivered
- the information you'll need
- what you will do
- what the client will do
- the contact person or persons
- confidentiality
- time schedule
- budget
- performance measures

Defining the Issues

There was no structured, well-defined problem when we started the study. The president just asked us to help him with "make vs. buy" decisions. Our original plan of action for field study research kept shifting as we interviewed more people and learned more about the company's capabilities and opportunities.

Our biggest problem was defining the scope of the project with our client at the outset. Once we had a clear definition of what it was they wanted, the project moved forward and progressed smoothly.

As these students found out, defining the issues to be worked on is often difficult. Almost invariably, the initial problem statement is symptomatic of deeper concerns. For example, the stated issue may be whether to market a new product through the direct sales force or the company's distributor channels; the underlying problem, however, may turn out to be the design and management of the company's distribution system. Or the failure of a new product launch may be perceived as an advertising and promotion problem, but in reality the issue is poor communication among the R&D, marketing, manufacturing, sales, and advertising functions and a breakdown in the product development and market introduction processes. Resolving such a problem may mean dealing with dysfunctional relationships among managers in several departments.

The client's initial problem statement can't be ignored, however, and the team may thus be working at two or three problem levels: (1) how to deal with what the client says is the problem, (2) how to define and deal with the underlying organizational and management issues that may have given rise to the problem, and (3) how to work around the politics of the situation to secure client commitment and corrective action.

Furthermore, client managers may be reluctant to express what is actually on their minds. If, for example, the key concern is the need for internal mediation, organizational development, or an evaluation of some functional unit, expressing such a concern may seem to them like "airing dirty linen." It should be kept in mind, as well, that any one manager's perceptions of the issues—and his or her ideas about solutions—will reflect the manager's own role biases and career interests.

It is also important for both the client and the team to have a clear understanding of what the job does not include. Potentially interesting areas of study may have to be left out because there simply isn't enough time for you to pursue them. It is essential to be realistic from the very beginning about what can be accomplished in the time you have and to be selective in deciding what particular contribution you can make.

The broader aspects of the problem may have to be left unsolved, as well, because departments and functions not under the client's scope of responsibility and authority would be involved. In addition, for internal political or competitive reasons, the client may not want outsiders to play a role in these matters at this time.

Finally, if you detect any expectations on the client's part that you will deliver certain things—e.g., proprietary information about competitors or candid evaluations of people in the client organization—that are unacceptable to you, you should state explicitly what you are not willing to do.

While issue definition—or project focus—is clearly of primary importance in a first-meeting agenda, constant reexamination is often necessary and should be prominent on the agenda of meetings with key client personnel. In the meantime, coming up with an explicit problem definition should not delay getting started on interviewing and other data gathering.

In general, the final problem statement should be able to satisfy the following criteria:

- It addresses both symptoms, as articulated by client managers, and causal factors, as developed in conversations among the managers and team members.

- The issue statement is mutually agreed upon by, and acceptable to, client managers, team members, and the faculty supervisor.
- The issue is of sufficient urgency to the client to ensure the client's full cooperation.
- The scope of the work is such that it can be accomplished in the time the team has available.
- The key client manager has the authority to give the team access to relevant file data and personnel who can contribute information and ideas essential for dealing with the issues.
- The problem is one on which action may feasibly be taken and solutions implemented within the scope of authority of client managers.
- Working on the issues will meet the team's goals for learning from field experience.
- The assignment does not involve team members, or client managers for that matter, in unethical activities.

The End Product

The contract should specify the nature of the product and to whom it will be delivered. Typically, the product consists of a written report and an oral presentation. Depending on the faculty supervisor's preferences and the wishes of client managers, it may be delivered in either one form or the other. In the case of a written report, it is essential to know at the outset who will receive copies and, for the oral presentation, who will be in attendance. This information helps focus the discussion in both reports.

The final report and/or written presentation are the client's property. Should any further use be made of the work (e.g., as a case study, or for inclusion in a faculty research project, or as a reference in an article or book), written approval for the intended use must be requested from the client organization. Finally, lest there be any doubt, it should be made explicit that all information the team receives during the course of the project will be treated as confidential, to be shared only among team members and their faculty supervisor.

Budgets

The major budget item is usually travel. Travel costs, of course, are a function of distance and the number of team-member days to be spent on field trips. In many projects, the budget must also provide for questionnaire surveys and/or focus group interviews. The budget should also include anticipated expenses for secretarial, duplicating, and graphics work. Finally, in the miscellaneous expenses category, provision should be made for telephone, postage, supplies, equipment rentals, and library literature searches.

Depending on the nature of the project and distances to be traveled, field studies project budgets usually run between $5,000 and $10,000, with reimbursements made for expenditures actually incurred. Developing a proposed budget is the responsibility of team members. Once they and the client managers agree on how the project will be carried out, obtaining client approval of project cost estimates generally does not pose problems; usually the client has a ballpark figure in mind at the outset. The faculty supervisor, on negotiating with sponsoring organizations, will often provide such a benchmark.

Problems in making cost reimbursements can arise if the client is restricted from making payments to individuals and proposes that such payments be made to your school. Government agencies and other nonprofit organizations sometimes face such restrictions.

The school's financial office may be precluded from acting as a transfer agent, i.e., accepting payments from sponsoring organizations and making payments to students. Thus, if reimbursement constraints do exist, the problem must be confronted as soon as possible and payment procedures worked out, usually with the help of the faculty supervisor.

Schedule

The contract should provide for one or two interim briefing meetings with key client managers before the final report is submitted. It would not be premature in the contracting meeting to set the date for the final oral presentation to ensure that those who should be there—particularly those managers who will have responsibility for taking any actions recommended in the report—have the date on their calendars.

Finally, team members may wish to schedule a debriefing on actions taken and the results six months or so after the conclusion of their work, to be conducted on-site, by a conference call, or by written communication. Reviewing what happened may enhance the learning experience for the team and benefit the client organization, particularly if there is opportunity for discussion.

Liaison Arrangements

Having one or more people from the company named to serve in a liaison capacity will be invaluable in facilitating the team's work. The contact person can be the go-between in scheduling meetings, making travel arrangements, and processing expense statements. This person can also be responsible for keeping a log of file memoranda and other reports used by the team as data sources. Whether more than one person is needed to fulfill this function depends on the individual project. In some instances, for example, different team members may be working in different departments in the client organization, and each may find it useful to have his or her own contact person. In some cases, the client may prefer to divide the different liaison tasks among different people. Normally, however, one contact person will suffice to coordinate team/client relationships.

Performance Measures

Finally, team members should raise questions about performance measures. What, exactly, does the client hope for? How will the client managers judge whether the project is a success from their perspective? What needs do they want the study to meet and for whom? Sometimes client managers can be vague about performance measures; to avoid misunderstandings later, team members should take some time to help them formulate and make explicit their expectations. The discussion may lead, moreover, to a more precise and realistic understanding of the issues to be covered and the needs of those who have a stake in the outcome.

Because no prescribed agenda can cover every relevant matter, it is useful to conclude the contracting meeting by asking client managers how they feel about the project so far and whether there are any matters not yet covered or any concerns not addressed. If the participants in the meeting have developed a rapport, some surprising and important concerns may arise:

- How much of our time will this take?
- Our ad agency gave us a report on this matter just a year ago; we're concerned that you may come out in a different place, and we don't want to rock the boat with the agency.
- My boss has some very positive views on what we should do about this problem, and I've got to deal with that if your recommendations aren't in line with her ideas.
- Manager X is a little nervous about this whole project; please be sensitive to that and see if you can get him aboard.

Such comments and questions may reflect misgivings about the project and the risks that managers may incur in being associated with it. It is far better to have such concerns emerge early than to have them lurking in the background and result in conflict and even resistance as the work proceeds.

Pitfalls

When asked in a questionnaire survey what their biggest problems were in dealing with sponsoring organizations, MBA students at Harvard Business School came up with the following observations:

Because of the dynamic nature of the company I felt that the company did not really know what it wanted us to do and was not prepared for the study. They also used us to fight internal political battles. We had difficulty or were unable to meet with some key figures we diligently tried to meet with.

The objective of the study was not clear to [Company X] in the beginning and was changed several times. This led to substantial delays in the beginning (2-4 weeks).

The target company was not on board, with the exception of one middle manager. We didn't have quality, up-to-date information from the target company, which would have made analysis more meaningful.

Agreement on the objectives; interaction with company and group was strained at times when the company was somewhat sensitive about our suggestions.

Political problems related to recommending something different from what was already implemented.

Distance and poor communications facilities; client responsiveness was slow; decision makers within the client organization were only moderately involved—the dominant attitude was that they were doing our school a favor, not that students were helping to solve an important matter.

Defining the nature of the problem and managing the expectations of the client and the faculty adviser.

Because this was an export project, access to overseas market information was difficult and expensive to obtain. One ten-day research trip overseas was sufficient but required extensive preparation. The company's cooperation was essential in order to make dealer appointments and to provide the field study team with credibility.

Change in field study direction halfway through project. This was managed successfully.

Getting interviews with key people in some of the companies. CEOs were tough to reach. Persistence was critical.

Senior management (not involved in initial meetings) felt that we didn't have the capabilities to do a proper study in West Germany and thought that we would use trips to the country as a vacation. Thus, our budget was cut, and the project scope narrowed one month into the project. The team had serious morale problems during the first several weeks of the project. It was too late to change projects, and we felt that [our client] didn't attach a high priority to our work. Our contact with senior man-

agement was extremely limited throughout the project, and we did our market study over the phone. It was a very frustrating experience.

Data Collection Methods

There are four basic sources of data for field projects: personal interviews, questionnaire surveys, focus group interviews, and the library archives. Personal interviews are almost always necessary, especially in the early stages of the work, and they often become the major vehicle for gathering facts and opinions.

Telephone and mail questionnaires may be used if the number of data points is too large and dispersed to access through personal interviews. Questionnaires are also necessary if the project calls for developing a statistically valid profile of some relevant group for purposes of describing preferences and behavior.

Focus group interviews are conducted with small groups of subjects who are representative of some target audience or constituency relevant to the client. Focus groups are used extensively to test new product ideas, to react to advertising themes and presentations, and to gather opinion on public policy issues.

Archival records—that is, library data—may be essential to tap in order to gain background context. Literature searches may be commissioned to find out, for example, about market size, competitors, product technology, relevant legislation, and publicly reported events of interest.

Written and Oral Reports

*T*he two most tangible products that come out of the field studies project are the written report and the oral presentation. Less tangible products, of course, are what students learn about an industry and/or a company and about how to do team study projects. Much client learning as well can take place over the course of the study.

The written and oral reports serve different purposes for the client, the faculty supervisor, and project team members; each offers different opportunities and constraints.

The written report should be a comprehensive document. It presents conclusions, recommendations, and action plans supported by qualitative and quantitative data. If client managers agree with what it says, they are likely to use it internally to persuade others to accept, and act on, its recommendations. Faculty supervisors will rely on the written report for evidence of creative thinking, the effective use of analytical tools and techniques, good research design, clear presentation, and the magnitude of the effort. The quality of the written report is a primary factor in assigning a grade.

There is no assurance, however, that the written report will be read by those whom the team wants to reach. For that reason, the document should be accessible and not forbidding in appearance.

The oral presentation provides a context for obtaining client acceptance of the recommendations, raising questions, dealing with resistance, and gaining commitment to take action. In addition, the quality of the oral presentation is, in most cases, an element in grading the study proj-

Note: This chapter was prepared by Professor E. Raymond Corey, Harvard Business School.

ect. The faculty supervisor will assess such factors as clarity of presentation, the quality of visual aids, and the team's effectiveness in managing the discussion. Finally, presenting the results of three or four months of intensive work can be immensely rewarding for students.

The inherent difficulties in making an oral presentation are time, audience attention span, and the potential for getting sidetracked if one or more of those present choose to engage in diversionary tactics. In addition, there is the risk of turning off the audience if the report is (1) dull and pedantic, (2) too crammed with facts and conclusions, or (3) given under adverse conditions, e.g., after lunch in a poorly lit or ventilated room. The keys to a successful oral presentation are to be extremely selective in choosing the information and ideas to be covered, to be patient but persistent in keeping the meeting on track, and to plan the meeting content and ambience to hold audience attention.

The oral presentation should not be an abridged version of the written report on which it is based. The messages to be delivered in the final meeting with the client must be selected according to exactly what the team wants to accomplish and, to be effective, should be tailored to the medium.

The Written Report

The written report should capture the totality of what the team has done over three or more months. This can be a blessing and a curse. On the one hand, the information is all there for client managers to use as they see fit, to serve as the basis for a grade, and, ideally, to remind project team members of a great experience. On the other hand, the temptation on the part of the writers to judge the accomplishment by its weight may lead to their including far more undigested data than would serve any of these purposes well.

To be useful, the written report must be well-organized, easily accessed through a table of contents, and crafted in clear and simple language. The reader should be able to track the line of argument from facts to analysis to conclusions to recommendations to action plans without difficulty.

Finally, to be convincing, the report should be objective. That is, it should leave the clear impression that the conclusions are based on sound evidence and that the project team has given fair consideration to all sides of any issue in its interpretation of the data.

Who's Going to See It?

The report should be addressed to the client manager identified as the senior person in whose area the study project falls and who has the responsibility and authority for taking action. It is important to remember, as well, that the report will be read by the faculty supervisor and could be circulated widely within the client organization. Thus, it must not be assumed that the readers have prior knowledge of the relevant background facts and circumstances. The document should be a complete statement that can be understood by someone unfamiliar with the problem, its context, or perhaps even salient facts about the industry setting.

At the same time, it is important to know to whom the client manager intends to disseminate the report: Who will be on the distribution list, and what limits will be set on how far it goes? This information is essential in judging whether to include certain confidential data and/or statements that might be sensitive in nature. Questions of confidentiality and sensitivity, as they apply to the contents of the written report, should be reviewed with the faculty supervisor and key members of the client organization when the report is in draft form.

Report Structure

A time-honored—and, yes, useful—tradition in business report writing is to begin with a one- or two-page executive summary. The summary should include a statement of the issues, key findings and conclusions, recommendations, and implementation steps. It may be followed by a table of contents outlining the body of the report. While the report structure will obviously vary depending on the nature of the project, the following topics should be covered:

- Project background
  - Why the study was undertaken
  - What issues were addressed; what potentially related aspects of the problem were not covered and why
  - Data sources
- Data analysis and conclusions
- Recommendations; consequences of taking or not taking action
- Implementation program
- Data appendixes

Writing Style

Any discussion of business report writing stresses the importance of using plain language, short sentences, and short paragraphs. In addition, the use of headings enhances readability. Indeed, having to organize the report by sections and subsections encourages clarity of thought and presentation.

Graphics—tables, bar charts, linear regressions, and pie charts, among others—can help readers grasp a point quickly and easily. Good graphics are simple and uncluttered. In addition, they should be numbered and explained in the text. The sources of exhibits should be duly noted, of course, both to give credit to their originator and to help the report reader judge the validity of any conclusions that may be drawn.

In the interest of clarity, brevity, and flow, appendixes and footnotes may be used to cover details not essential to the main line of argument but useful for reference purposes. For example, if a questionnaire survey was used to gather data, the survey form and a tabulation of the results might be included in an appendix to support the observations and conclusions contained in the main body of the text.

Finally, the report's conclusions must be supported by facts. Facts alone have no value unless they lead to analysis, interpretations, conclusions, and recommendations. A good report-writing technique is to begin paragraphs and/or sections of the report by stating conclusions and then backing them up with factual observations. The report will be especially convincing if both sides of an issue are considered and the reader does not detect bias because essential facts have been omitted or the data interpretation has been slanted.

The Writing Process

Well before the data-gathering phase of the project is completed, team meetings—brainstorming sessions—should be scheduled to review and analyze the findings. The goals of these meetings are to reach tentative conclusions and identify gaps in the data. At the same time, the team should check its emerging conclusions and recommendations with its faculty supervisor and, in addition, schedule an interim reporting meeting with key client managers. The input from both meetings may lead to making some mid-course corrections. More important, meetings with the faculty supervisor and client managers will show them the direction the study is taking and ensure that the final report will contain no unwelcome surprises. An interim briefing meeting usually serves, as well, to give client managers a sense of ownership of the emerging ideas and enables them to begin to build internal support for the recommendations they anticipate receiving.

As team meetings continue, the broad structure of a report will emerge, based on key areas of analysis. Team members may then construct an outline with numbered major and sub headings. A next step might be to code the data that have been gathered and to list next to each heading on the outline the document and page references that pertain to that item. Student members can then review the outline, seeking agreement on what data are relevant, the conclusions to be drawn, and the recommendations that follow.

Usually, every team member is involved in writing the first draft of the report, with each student responsible for doing certain sections. Section drafts may then be reviewed in regularly scheduled team meetings and taken back for revision. It is advisable, however, to have one team member prepare the final draft to eliminate repetition and to ensure consistency of style. Finally, it is often useful to have your faculty supervisor or some disinterested party—a person not associated with the project—read the report for clarity and cohesiveness—if such a step is not a breach of confidence.

The writing process is inevitably slow, and any temptation to prolong the data-gathering stage at the risk of cutting short writing time should be resisted.

The Oral Presentation

The feedback meeting, in which the project team makes its final report to client managers, is the "moment of truth"—a time for seeing how the team's ideas "fly," for defending the team's conclusions and observations in the face of possible skepticism, and for gaining recognition for a job well done. It should be approached as a "production." That means having a clear sense at the outset of what messages the team wants to get across, the agenda from start to finish, the staging (e.g., room set-up, the use of visuals), and presentation style. Knowing who will be present, team members should take time before the meeting to anticipate and plan responses to client manager reactions, possible questions, and sources of resistance. Careful planning will pay off handsomely.

Who Will Be There?

Attendance at the final meeting with the client should have been discussed earlier to ensure the team that the "right" people will be on hand to hear its final report. The key objectives of the meeting are: (1) to win acceptance for, and support of, the conclusions and recommendations, (2) to deal with any misunderstandings, questions, and objections, and (3) to gain commitment for taking action. In addition, at the close of the meeting, team members may want to express interest in learning, at some later date, about the results of actions taken.

Knowing who will be there is important for another reason: it allows team members to take audience dynamics into account in planning their presentation. Some client managers may typically defer to others. Some may be inclined to raise objections if others react approvingly. Some may feel threatened while others feel supported by the team's recommendations. Some may fear that the oral report implies personal criticism.

Being sensitive to audience dynamics is essential in planning how to present your message. Ideally, there should be no losers coming out of a study project; the team's report should generate unanimous and enthusiastic endorsement. That can happen, and constructive action can follow, if everybody goes away with a sense of winning.

The Agenda

A common failing in planning the oral report is to use most of the time available for the presentation and to leave insufficient time for discussion and responding to questions. Remember that the object of this exercise is to have managers "go on the line" in committing to doing something, to elicit questions and reservations, and to get feedback as part of the learning experience. These goals cannot be accomplished if the team uses the entire meeting to present the results of its work. It is essential, then, to plan how you want to use the time you will have well before the meeting takes place.

While the meeting may be informal and allow for questions and comments at any time, it is important that the agenda be controlled with respect both to timing and substance. One project team member should assume responsibility for moving along the presentation and discussion, gently but firmly, to avoid running out of time. In addition, he or she or the presenters must keep questions and comments focused on key issues—again, being tactful and firm but still responding to the needs of those present to have their views heard. Not easy. Managing the feedback meeting calls for thinking on one's feet.

The Meeting Room

Whether the presentation meeting is to be held on campus or in client organization offices, team members should have the opportunity to inspect the space ahead of time. Does it have chalkboards, a projection screen, flip charts? Is the room well lighted? Can the room temperature be easily regulated? How are the acoustics? Will everybody be able to see the presenters clearly and to read the printing on slides and flip charts easily?

Good lighting is essential. It is a particularly relevant consideration in choosing between vugraph slides or 35 mm color transparencies for visuals. Generally, the use of the latter requires that the room be darkened; vugraph slides may usually be seen clearly with only the projection screen in the shade.

Using Visuals

Visuals can be used effectively to provide an outline from which the speaker may talk and to help the audience follow the flow of the presentation. Using the slides as prompts, presenters may be less formal, freer to use "body language"—better able to hold audience attention and to engage client managers in discussion than if they were speaking from a prepared text. The most important thing to remember is that the visuals are there to *support* the speaker, not to make the speech. The audience should be looking at and listening to you, not trying to read and decipher a plethora of visual images.

For every slide or overhead, consider what the main point is and how best to highlight that point visually. Then express it with headings that are clear, short, and easily read. How the text is organized through heads, bullets, highlighting, and "menu" slides is important, as is the effective arrangement of essential data in tables, and the proper choice of graphic display modes, e.g., bar charts, pie charts, linear regressions.

The single most common problem with slides is overcrowding. Copy should be concise and written in an abbreviated, outline style. Data should be simplified as much as possible. For data too voluminous for a single slide, consider summarizing the material or splitting it into two or more slides. A rule of thumb: three bullets per slide.

Fewer is better; remember the audience's tendency to "glaze over" after too many visuals, especially where there are several presenters.

Headings: make them interesting—a statement, a major idea, or a provocative question. Upper and lower case text is much easier on the eye than all capital letters.

Slides or overheads? Overheads give the speaker greater flexibility to skip ahead if time is short and to go back to earlier overheads in response to questions. And as noted above, the light level in the room may be higher when using overheads—an important consideration in holding audience attention.

The following exhibits are examples of effective graphics. Note the following:

Exhibit 2-1: Three bullets only; each a clear idea.

Exhibit 2-2: A question/answer format.

Exhibit 2-3: The "What's New" heading provides an organizing marker.

Note: The ideas in the section "Using Visuals" were contributed by Mary Ellen Gardner, Publications Manager, Harvard Business School.

Exhibit 2-4: Simple, clear, easy-to-read graphics. The scales on each axis are not crowded.

Exhibit 2-5: A flow diagram with about the maximum number of boxes for easy reading. The type size is good relative to the box size.

Exhibit 2-6: Pie chart; note that the labels for the smaller slices are outside the circle.

Exhibit 2-1

**Confused Accountabilities
Consequences:**

- Lack of clear purpose on boards
- Confused discussions
- Directors often feel forced to do "The Wrong Thing"

Exhibit 2-2

Who Develops Strategy and Structure?

Traditional   ⟶   Top management
organization

Decentralized   ⟶   Upper levels
organization

Self-designing   ⟶   All levels
organization

Exhibit 2-3

What's New

Large Distributors' Increasing Share of Resale $

	mid '70s	mid '80s
Electronics components 10 largest distributors	37%	55%
Hospital supplies 6 largest distributors	23%	55%

Exhibit 2-4

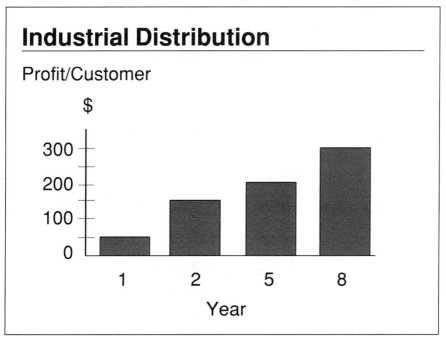

Industrial Distribution

Profit/Customer

Exhibit 2-5

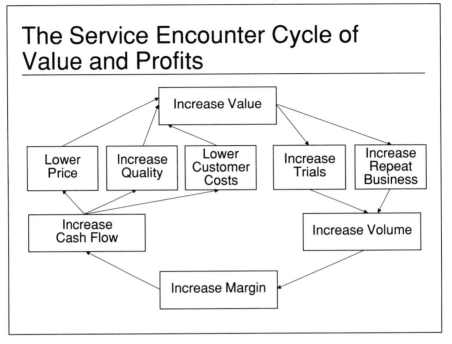

Exhibit 2-6

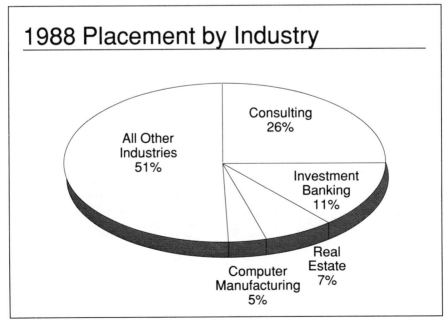

Making the Presentation

Project team members usually remember the final meeting with the client and their presentation before key client managers as a challenging climax to a long stretch of intensive work. Going in with feelings of anxiety and apprehension, team members often come out with a high sense of accomplishment and reward, a sense that the total effort was most worthwhile. Here are some thoughts on helping to make the final meeting a success.

Style—An oral presentation should sound more like a conversation than an essay. Because the style of most business presentations is slightly less formal than written prose, you want to be careful not to fall back into a written style when you write the speech. Think of yourself as speaking to a friend and say the sentences aloud as you write them.

Length—A good rule of thumb is to have less material than you think you need. You don't want to run long, and no audience has ever complained that a speech was too short.

Rehearsing—Rehearse the entire speech each time you practice. Rehearse out loud and, if possible, in front of a friend.

If you are not going to memorize your whole speech, at least memorize the opening and closing remarks. Your credibility with the audience is most important at the beginning and end of your speech. Speaking directly to them without notes will allow you to make eye contact.

Body Language—Gestures can be an important part of a speech. But rather than worry about where to put your hands, try to forget about them entirely and they'll act like hands rather than unnatural appendages. The same goes for your feet—a little natural movement is better than rigidity. Indeed, moving from one spot to another when you change topics can serve as a kind of visual punctuation.

Remember to play to all parts of the room. Eye contact is important. However, if you see people sleeping or scowling, don't try to win them over. Look somewhere else for a more encouraging face.

Notes—NEVER read your speech and never bring the fully written document with you. Reading a speech creates distance between you and the audience. While you may tell yourself the written copy is there just in case your memory goes, it will be too tempting to sneak a glance and then another, until you're hooked.

Using no notes is best, but most people find a few notes comforting. Because paper rattles and more than two pages become cumbersome,

---

Note: The section "Making the Presentation" was adapted from "A Note on Oral Presentations," HBS No. 9-486-108 by Sally Seymour, Associate in Communication, Harvard Business School.

most speakers prefer 3x5 cards. On the cards you should have the main point in a phrase or word, and something to get you to the next card. Your cues can also be written on the frames of your vugraph slides.

Order of Speakers—There are several ways to allocate the tasks in a team presentation where everyone is to speak. The most obvious division is to have each person speak on the area he or she researched. However, it's also useful to consider strengths and weaknesses. Some people are better at handling visual aids and should take that part of the speech where such aids are most prevalent; some have a greater problem with nervousness and should be allowed to speak early; the two people with the strongest presentation skills would be most strategically placed first and last where persuasiveness counts.

Transitions—Without smooth transitions between speakers and subjects, group presentations appear disrupted and disorganized. In addition to introducing the topic, the first speaker should introduce the other speakers by name and, briefly, the area each will cover. Then, each succeeding speaker should also provide a transition to the next one by saying something like "and now, Bill will tell you about _____." At the end, the last speaker should provide a summary of the whole presentation.

Question and Answer—A problem with the question-and-answer period is maintaining your control of the forum. During the speech you are in charge, but you lose that authority when you give over the floor to someone else. One way to keep control is to rephrase the question in your own words and then to give your answer not just to the questioner, but to the whole room.

Giving an oral presentation, either as part of a group or alone, can be a most anxiety-arousing experience. Unfortunately, it is that very anxiety that threatens the success of the presentation: the more nervous you are, the more nervous you become because you're afraid the nervousness will cause you to fail.

One way of reducing fear of failure is to be exceptionally well-prepared. Nervousness is a lapse in concentration; instead of having your whole mind centered on what you are saying, part of it is off criticizing your performance. However, if you've rehearsed a sufficient number of times, you should be able to carry through by rote until you can get your concentration back to where it belongs. Wandering concentration is a problem even for professional speakers, but the more experienced you become, the quicker you'll be able to get it back.

Someone once calculated that 75% of a successful presentation is preparation, 15% breathing technique, 5% exercises (tension relievers like neck rolls), and 5% psyching yourself up for it. Guests waiting to appear on television talk shows are encouraged to repeat silently to themselves phrases like "Everyone loves me" or "I know more about this subject than anyone." Silly as it sounds, people claim it works.

Accept the fact that nervousness is natural. It's a good idea to avoid coffee or tea, especially on an empty stomach. The caffeine may combine with the adrenaline that's already shooting through your system to give you a case of the shakes. If your throat tends to get dry and constricted when you get nervous, take a cup of warm water on stage with you. Warm liquid is better than cold since it relaxes the stomach as well as the throat muscles.

A FINAL AND POSSIBLY ENCOURAGING NOTE: People tend to think they're better writers and worse speakers than they actually are.

3

Field Interviews

*P*ersonal interviewing is the primary methodology for structuring the project and for gathering essential facts and opinions about the issues, historical background, problem symptoms and causes, and possible solutions. Personal interviews are used, as well, to probe the relationships surrounding the problem: how the work is organized, systems in use, how people interact, and performance measures—either explicit or implicit—that condition behavior. Further, personal interviewing is probably the most effective way to gain an understanding of how the issues affect client personnel and what their stakes, as individuals, are in the outcome of the project.

Structured Versus Nondirective Interviewing

Should the interview be structured or nondirective? A structured interview follows a predetermined set of questions. A nondirective approach allows for flexibility in the discussion, relying on the interviewee to volunteer relevant facts and opinions, with broad guidance from the interviewer. Tightly structured interviews come close to becoming questionnaire surveys administered in person. They may be useful if the interviewer has a clear sense of precisely what the issues are and what information is needed to work toward a solution. The narrower the issue and the more sharply focused the data search, the more useful structured

Note: This chapter was prepared by Professor E. Raymond Corey, Harvard Business School.

interviews become. Even under these conditions, drafting a relevant and comprehensive set of questions usually requires that you conduct non-directive interviews in the early stages of the project to determine the problem focus and to specify the data needed.

In unstructured—that is, nondirective—interviews, the project team member is soliciting the cooperation of the interviewee in developing a database of useful information. A cooperative interviewee often offers facts and opinions that go beyond what the interviewer may have thought to elicit through structured questioning; new perspectives and new lines of inquiry are thus opened.

Unstructured interview techniques, however, do not prevent the interviewer from using specific questions. On the contrary, the interviewee usually expects to be queried and may perceive the interview to be a "fishing expedition" if the discussion is too open-ended. Specific questions are useful to begin the conversation and, if broadly formulated, to provide guidance for the interviewee.

Interview Guidelines

The following guidelines obviously do not apply to every situation but, taken together, they may help project team members to prepare for meetings with client personnel and others who can provide useful data.

Make the interviewee comfortable:

- Describe the project and the issues as you understand them.
- Say why you picked this project; what you hope to gain from it.
- Show an interest in the company, the topic, the interviewee, and his or her background.
- Show that you have done some homework on the company and the industry.
- Raise factual questions that are relevant but not sensitive.
- Don't show superior knowledge and/or ideas about how issues may be resolved.

Help the interviewee feel secure:

- Indicate that any information given in confidence will be so treated.
- Offer to submit notes of the interview to the interviewee for review, correction, and elaboration.
- Don't quote previous interviewees or ask the interviewee to comment on what they said if there is any risk of passing on information and opinions given in confidence.

Ask about:

- The interviewee's perceptions of the issues; background factors; the interviewee's suggestions for resolving the issues.
- How the interviewee experiences the issues and how they affect his or her work or department.

Listen for:

- Clues on other sources of relevant information, e.g., "We made a study of that a while ago"; "We get into that in our annual plans statement"; "There's some good data in the industry trade association reports."
- Tips on who else in the organization can contribute additional information and especially divergent opinions, e.g., "Of course the manufacturing guys don't agree with us."
- What's mentioned more than once either by the same person or by different people in the organization and ask why, e.g., "You've mentioned this a couple of times; could you tell me why it is especially significant?"
- Both implicit and explicit assumptions and evaluative comments, e.g., "The way things work in this company. . ."; "As a rule, distributors can't be counted on to do market development . . ."
- What the interviewee thinks is critical. Ask why these points are important.
- Interpretations, evaluative comments, beliefs, and explanations about the way things were, are, and/or should be. Whether they are factually accurate may not be important; what is important is that these may be perceptions that shape the way the interviewee thinks and acts.
- Indications of the interviewee's values, e.g., "Customers come first"; "We really have to protect the older workers"; "We're becoming a lot more bureaucratic; it's killing initiative and taking a lot of fun out of working here."
- What the interviewee is *not* saying, that is, presumably avoiding or cannot say without help.

Understand what is being said:

- Be sensitive to the interview context. The interviewee may consciously or subconsciously
  - · say what he or she wants you to hear, or
  - · be on guard for fear of being evaluated by the interviewer and/or other persons in the room, or
  - · be concerned about conveying information that may damage the interviewee's position in the company.

- Be aware of how the person's background experiences and current role interests will influence the information he or she does and doesn't communicate, perceptions of the problem, and suggestions for action.
- Look for patterns; put what you are hearing in a frame of reference. Listen for things that relate to, amplify, confirm, or are consistent with what other people have said. Probe further.
- Be particularly aware of comments that don't fit some emerging pattern and try to understand apparent inconsistencies. Be prepared, in that case, to reformulate the issues, problem analysis, and tentative recommendations.

Conduct the interview in a nonobtrusive manner:

- Listen in a patient, friendly but intelligently probing manner; be sure to show interest in what is being said.
- Don't argue with the speaker.
- Put the speaker in a position of authority.
- Talk or ask questions only to
    - · open the interview
    - · direct the conversation to another topic area
    - · discuss the significance of what is being said
    - · help the person talk
    - · relieve any anxieties on the speaker's part that may be affecting the interview
- Don't put words in the speaker's mouth or suggest interpretations of what is being said to suit your own ideas.
- Get the speaker to extend and elaborate on what he or she said with questions like, "I don't understand that; could you help me?"
- Ask for concrete examples.
- Avoid frequent interruptions; flag your questions on your notepad and wait for a lull in the conversation to go back to them.
- Don't express value judgments or opinions about what the interviewee is telling you about himself or herself, or about other people, or about actions taken or not taken.
- Don't offer advice, but if it's solicited, be cautious and tentative in your response.
- Express appreciation for the interviewee's time, factual information, and insights.

At the end of the interview, keep "a foot in the door" with a comment such as, "May I get back to you if I have any questions?" or "I'd like to send you a copy of my notes and then call you to get any suggestions you might have for corrections or added information." Second-round interviewing, if time permits, can be especially valuable, particularly if the interviewee has been given the first-round notes. The interviewee is likely to feel more secure and more comfortable with the interviewer in a second meeting and be more open. Furthermore, after reviewing the record of the initial meeting, the interviewee is likely to think of other useful and relevant information and/or sources of information to pass on to the interviewer.

Taking Notes

The above guidelines suggest that the interviews will be largely nondirective or, at the least, loosely guided by the interviewer. In unstructured interviewing, note taking may be done by hand or through a tape recorder or both. Tape recording has the obvious advantage of providing a more complete record, one that can be reviewed later at leisure. The disadvantage, if any, lies in any apprehension it may create in the interviewee, inhibiting the free flow of comments.

Written note taking is usually seen as less obtrusive but the interviewer needs to write fast and to work later from rough notes to prepare an elaborated interview record. If more than a day passes between the interview and writing a file memorandum of it, the interviewer risks losing the recall to reconstruct the conversation accurately from his or her rough notes. Especially if note taking is by hand, having two interviewers—double teaming—is valuable for alternating between interrogating the interviewee and recording what is being said.

How do you know when your data collecting is done? Generally, you're finished when you are beginning to hear the same things over and over again. If that is not happening before it's time to begin writing your report and preparing an oral presentation, then it may be well to narrow the scope of the project and go with what data you've got. In any case, do not underestimate the amount of time you'll need for sifting through the inevitably voluminous data you will have accumulated, doing the analysis, and writing up the results.

4

Using Library Resources

As you undertake your field studies project, you will, of course, spend much of your time gathering data from original sources—for example, through interviews and surveys. The project will benefit as well from information gained through library research. Secondary sources found in a business library can provide valuable background information on industries and companies, and point the way to primary sources outside the library.

Like any research, business research is both exciting and frustrating. Information can be elusive; promising leads may turn into dead ends. Carefully planning your research strategy and arming yourself with a few tools can help make the task less formidable and more rewarding.

Research is inevitably a learning process, but it helps to benefit from the experience of others; here are some useful tips to keep in mind:

1. By determining at the outset exactly what sort of data you need, you will save a great deal of time throughout the course of the study. For example, is the information you need historical or current? Is it specific to an industry, a company, or a country? Is it primarily economic, political, demographic, or biographical?

   General business reference books can answer some of these questions, but more specific references would be more appropriate. While the *U.S. Statistical Abstract* is a valuable resource for statistics collected by the U.S. government, the *Survey of Current Business* is the resource to use when you need monthly data or more recent statistics. *Moody's Transportation Manual* can be used for

Note: This chapter was prepared by Sue Marsh, Corporate Information Librarian, and Erika McCaffrey, Reference Department Head, Baker Library, Harvard Business School.

information on companies in the transportation industry, while *Automotive News* is the place to start for current information on the automotive industry. A thorough knowledge of library resources or planning a strategy with a business reference librarian can save hours, if not days.

Exhibit 4-1 lists types of data by industry, company, country, and economic issues. The information sources corresponding to these categories can usually be found in business libraries. Consult with a librarian to identify those most appropriate for your needs.

2. Try to obtain information from as close to the source as possible. Trade associations, local newspapers, press releases, and embassies are invaluable resources. SEC (Securities and Exchange Commission) data, which are filed by corporations and are publicly available, provide broad and detailed coverage. SEC documents include the *Annual Report to Stockholders* (graphics, narrative, and financial statements), the *Proxy Statement* (notice of annual meeting and background on matters to be voted upon), the *Prospectus* (notice and details of new stock issues), and Form 10-K (detailed financial information, lists of subsidiaries, and information on ownership and management).

3. When using a reference book, be sure to read the introduction to determine the book's focus; it is not always clear from the title. Carefully reading introductions will show you why, for example, only 1,000 public companies were included in one directory and 12,000 were included in another.

4. Be wary of the accuracy of printed data. Information may become dated even as a document is being printed. A daily newspaper will be more accurate than an annual directory.

5. While the *Reader's Guide to Periodical Literature* is an excellent tool for identifying articles in magazines and journals, it is not the only periodical index and is not always appropriate for graduate-level research. There are many specialized indexes that may offer more comprehensive listings on a particular subject.

6. No single resource will cover a subject in its entirety. Do not assume that a directory of banks will include all banks or that a periodical index on insurance will list all articles about insurance.

7. The source of a statistic (usually printed at the bottom of a table) is as important as the statistic itself to establish validity as well as limitations. For example, statistics on the tobacco industry issued by the American Cancer Society might differ from those issued by the American Tobacco Institute. While both sets of statistics may be accurate, they may also reflect the particular bias of the group.

8. Journals are often indexed for the previous year either in the last issue of the volume or in the first issue of the next volume. If one

Exhibit 4-1

Research Questions

Industry Data
- Competitors
- Market Size/Growth
- Market Forecasts
- Market Segmentation
- Pricing
- M&A Statistics
- Ratios
- Technology
- Domestic vs. International
- Recent Developments
- Industry Expectations

Company Data
- Public/Private
- Profitability
- Portfolio/Structure
- Products/Services
- Market Share
- Balance Sheet
- Stock Price
- Costs
- Facilities
- Employees
- Ownership
- Biography
- M&A History
- Analyst Expectations

Economic Data
- Population/Demographic
- Trends/Indices
- Business Patterns
- Cost of Living
- GNP

Country Data
- Trade
- Exchange Rates
- Legislation
- General

journal is key to your research, it may be faster to search that journal's index rather than an index covering many different journals.

9. Ask for help when you need it.

Librarians

Speaking with a librarian at the beginning of the field study will help you determine what type of information will be most relevant for your project and how to plan your research. (It is usually best to telephone ahead to schedule an appointment.) Some librarians specialize in business information sources and can help plan search strategies and brainstorm solutions to problems. Since they know the resources in their libraries, they can often save you time by targeting the best reference sources.

Computerized Literature Searches

Computerized literature searches can be conducted on a range of topics, from history to current events to biography. Two types of searches are available: those conducted by the researcher on compact discs (e.g., *ABI/Inform*, *Compustat PC-Plus*, and *Lotus OneSource CD/Corporate*) and those conducted by a librarian. There is usually no charge for using CD-ROM databases.

Information obtained from a CD search is most efficiently saved on a disk. When planning to use a CD, be sure to check ahead to see what size disk will be needed.

Information searches done by a librarian are often more efficient than do-it-yourself CD searches. Librarians will know quickly what databases are relevant and what search strategies most appropriate. These searches usually carry a fee; since the costs of databases vary, you should discuss fees with the librarian before submitting your budget for approval.

Public Versus Private Companies

When looking for corporate financial data, the first question to ask is whether the company is publicly or privately held. Since privately held firms are not required to disclose financial information, few resources will be available. Business directories, such as *Ward's Business Directory of U.S. Private and Public Companies,* may offer some information. *Dun's Credit Searches* provides financial information on any company that has borrowed money, floated bonds, or offered stock publicly. Access to these credit listings is limited to companies and libraries that subscribe to this on-line access service.

Publicly held companies are required to disclose financial data and news of material events on a regular basis to stockholders and to the SEC. They do so through such documents as annual reports to stockholders, proxy statements, prospectuses, SEC filings on forms 10K and 10Q, and registration statements. These reports contain balance sheets, income statements, descriptions of new stock or bond issues, updates on changes in corporate ownership, the auditor's report, information on subsidiaries, and management discussions. These documents are available from the companies themselves, from the SEC, and from the microfiche and CD-ROM vendors. CD-ROM databases, such as *Lotus One Source CD/Corporate,* Disclosure's *Compact Disclosure,* and Standard & Poor's *Compact PC-Plus,* draw on information derived from SEC filings and present it along with other information.

Directories

Business directories generally list companies in a particular field and provide brief descriptions of them. Researchers consult directories to find addresses, telephone numbers, officers, and principal lines of business. Most directories index their contents geographically, by industry and/or product, and alphabetically by company name. Some index companies by sales size, number of employees, and officer names as well. A researcher may use these directories and ranked lists to identify competitors, to target companies in a geographic region, and/or to compile mailing lists for a particular demographic segment.

The scope of a directory is also important. In addition to general business directories such as *Standard & Poor's Register* and *Moody's Manuals,* there are hundreds of geographic or industry-specific directories. *Japan Trade Directory,* the *Massachusetts Service Directory, Pratt's Guide to Venture Capital Sources,* the *Directory of Management Consultants,* and *Thomas Register of American Manufacturers* are but a few. *Directories in Print* is an invaluable guide to business directories.

In addition, more and more directories are being produced on compact discs and are available on-line through database vendors. A business librarian or information broker can guide the researcher to libraries with CDs or search the directories on-line.

Periodical Indexes

Periodical indexes that focus on business include *A.B.A. Banking Literature Index, Business Periodicals Index, Predicasts F & S Index United States, The Financial Times Index,* and *Computer Literature Index.* Most follow the same format, with citations of articles arranged by major subject heading. Each has particular strengths, depending on the researcher's needs. *The Wall Street Journal Index* and the *Predicasts Indexes,* for example, may be especially useful because they contain separate indexes by company name. Many indexes, such as *ABI/Inform* and *Business Periodicals Index,* are now being produced in electronic format and are useful for more complex searches. There are additional indexes produced on-line available through such vendors as Dialog and BRS.

Journals and Newspapers

General business magazines and newspapers such as *Business Week, Fortune,* and the *Wall Street Journal* are meant for a broad readership. While these periodicals usually provide useful background information, they are often too general for the researcher. Virtually every field of business, however, has its own journals or newspapers that spot trends long before they are noticed in the general business literature. You can quickly identify the important journals in a particular field by noting which journals are usually cited in the literature. Examples of journals with particular readerships in mind are *Institutional Investor, J.A.S.A.* (the *Journal of the American Statistical Association*), and *Advertising Age.*

Industry and Company Analyses

Before studying detailed company statistics and profiles, you may want to review an industry analysis. These analyses offer background information, profiles, and forecasts for particular industries. A valuable source of industry information is the U.S. Department of Commerce's annual *U.S. Industrial Outlook.* It covers 350 industries, with a strong em-

phasis on manufacturing and mining. Another source is *Standard &
Poor's Industry Surveys,* which covers fewer industries than the *U.S. Industrial Outlook,* although the retail and service industries are better rep-
resented.

Wall Street analysts' reports are a highly regarded source for both industry and public-company analysis. Written from an investment perspective, these reports contain financial data as well as information on
trends, markets, and future prospects. Most libraries do not carry
analysts' reports, however, since they are intended for brokerage houses'
customers. Most libraries do have access to the Investext database
and/or the brokerage reports on the NEXIS system, which contain the
full text of major Wall Street analysts' reports. To identify Wall Street analysts by specialty, consult *Nelson's Directory of Investment Research. Lotus
OneSource CD/Corporate* includes portions of the Investext database. Ad-
ditionally, some libraries may have microfiche collections of analysts' reports produced by *Corporate Information Research Reports (CIRR).*

Market research reports are usually produced privately by corporations or research firms; if and when they are released, they are very expensive. A good subject index of these reports is *Findex: The Directory of
Market Research Reports, Studies and Surveys.*

Ratios

Financial and operating ratios are excellent sources of information for
analyzing both public and private companies. Most sources for financial
ratios show industry averages by SIC (Standard Industrial Classification)
code. In addition to profitability and solvency ratios, average balance
sheets can usually be found. The three best-known sources of financial
ratios are Dun's *Industry Norms and Key Business Ratios, Robert Morris Associates Statement Studies,* and *Troy's Almanac of Business and Industrial Ratios.* Since each provides different information, more than one title may
need to be consulted.

Ranked Lists

Lists of companies ranked by sales, assets, or employees can help target larger companies as well as competitors in an industry. Most major
company directories have general ranked lists of companies, as well as
industry groupings. Magazines such as *Forbes, Fortune, Business Week,*
and *Inc.* compile annual rankings. Many other smaller trade publica-

tions rank companies within an industry or geographic area. A good source for identifying ranked lists by subject is *Business Rankings Annual*.

Stock Prices

There are many ways to locate stock prices, depending on how recent the prices need to be and whether they need to be daily, weekly, monthly, or annual. Much of this information is available on-line through Compustat, CRSP, and Dow Jones, to name a few. Print sources are also available, and a business librarian should be consulted as to which one best fits the needs of frequency, timeliness, and historical coverage.

Government Documents

U.S. government documents offer a wealth of information for the field studies researcher, ranging from business censuses to household demographics. Most of the information dealing with population, employment, wages, economic data, cost of living, and import/export is statistical. The best way to track down these documents is by consulting the *U.S. Statistical Abstract*. The Census Bureau produces written reports on population trends that cover topics such as working mothers. International government documents supply similar information on a worldwide and country-by-country basis.

The International Monetary Fund, United Nations, Organisation for Economic Cooperation and Development (O.E.C.D), and Eurostat are the major publishers. Indexes such as *American Statistics Index (ASI)* or *Statistical Reference Index (SRI)* will help identify the appropriate source by subject. Government documents can be confusing and hard to use; assistance from a business librarian can save time and prevent frustration.

Trade Associations

Trade associations are sometimes the only source of information in a highly specialized industry. Many groups maintain research departments, and some have extensive libraries. Not all associations will share information with nonmembers, but they are usually worth contacting. Many associations publish newsletters, statistics, and directories. Publications information, membership, and contact information are available in the Encyclopedia of Associations.

References

INDUSTRY

ABI/Inform. [On-line database and CD-ROM.] Ann Arbor, MI: University Microfilms International. Weekly [on-line], monthly [CD-ROM].

American Statistics Index. Washington, DC.: Congressional Information Service, monthly.

Business Periodicals Index. New York: The H.W. Wilson Company, monthly.

Business Rankings Annual. Detroit, MI: Gale Research Inc., annual.

Corporate Information Research Reports (CIRR). [Microfiche collection, on-line database, and CD-ROM database.] East Chester, NY: J.A. Micropublishing, monthly.

Compact Disclosure. [CD-ROM database.] Bethesda, MD: Disclosure Incorporated, monthly.

Compustat. [Computer tape files and CD-ROM database.] New York: Standard & Poor's Compustat Services, Inc., weekly.

Directories in Print. Detroit, MI: Gale Research Inc., annual.

Encyclopedia of Associations. Detroit, MI: Gale Research Inc., annual.

Findex: The Directory of Market Research Reports, Studies and Surveys. New York: Cambridge Information Group Directories, Inc., semiannual.

Lotus OneSource. [CD-ROM database.] Cambridge, MA: Lotus Development Corporation, monthly.

Nelson's Directory of Investment Research. Port Chester, NY: W.R. Nelson & Co./Nelson Publications, annual.

Predicasts Indexes. Cleveland, OH: Predicasts, biweekly.

Robert Morris Associates Annual Statement Studies. Lansdowne, PA: Robert Morris Associates, annual.

Standard & Poor's Industry Surveys. New York: Standard & Poor's Corporation, irregular.

Statistical Reference Index. Washington, DC: Congressional Information Service, bimonthly.

Thomas Register of American Manufacturers. New York: Thomas Publishing Company, annual.

United States Department of Commerce. *U.S. Industrial Outlook.* Washington, DC: Government Printing Office, annual.

Value Line Investment Survey. New York: Value Line Publishing, Inc., weekly.

Ward's Business Directory of U.S. Private and Public Companies. Detroit, MI: Gale Research Inc., annual.

COMPANY

ABI/Inform. [On-line database and CD-ROM.] Ann Arbor, MI: University Microfilms International. Weekly [on-line], monthly [CD-ROM].

Business Periodicals Index. New York: The H.W. Wilson Company, monthly.

Business Rankings Annual. Detroit, MI: Gale Research Inc., annual.

Corporate Information Research Reports (CIRR). [Microfiche collection, on-line database, and CD-ROM database.] East Chester, NY: J.A. Micropublishing, monthly.

Compact Disclosure. [CD-ROM database.] Bethesda, MD: Disclosure Incorporated, monthly.

Compustat. [Computer tape files and CD-ROM database.] New York: Standard & Poor's Compustat Services, Inc., weekly.

Directories in Print. Detroit, MI: Gale Research Inc., annual.

Directory of Corporate Affiliations. Wilmette, IL: National Register Publishing Company, annual.

Encyclopedia of Associations. Detroit, MI: Gale Research Inc., annual.

Findex: The Directory of Market Research Reports, Studies and Surveys. New York: Cambridge Information Group Directories, Inc., semiannual.

International Directory of Corporate Affiliations. Wilmette, IL: National Register Publishing Company, annual.

Lotus OneSource. [CD-ROM database.] Cambridge, MA: Lotus Development Corporation, monthly.

Moody's Manuals. 7 volumes. New York: Moody's Investors Service, weekly.

Nelson's Directory of Investment Research. Port Chester, NY: W.R. Nelson & Co./Nelson Publications, annual.

Predicasts Indexes. Cleveland, OH: Predicasts, biweekly.

Reference Book of Corporate Managements. New York: Dun's Marketing Services, Inc., annual.

Thomas Register of American Manufacturers. New York: Thomas Publishing Company, annual.

Value Line Investment Survey. New York: Value Line Publishing, Inc., weekly.

Ward's Business Directory of U.S. Private and Public Companies. Detroit, MI: Gale Research Inc., annual.

ECONOMIC

ABI/Inform. Ann Arbor, MI: University Microfilms International. [On-line database and CD-ROM.] Weekly [on-line], monthly [CD-ROM].

Business Periodicals Index. New York: The H.W. Wilson Company, monthly.

Predicasts Indexes. Cleveland, OH: Predicasts, biweekly.

Survey of Buying Power. New York: Sales & Marketing Management, annual.

United States Department of Commerce. *Survey of Current Business.* Washington, DC: Government Printing Office, monthly.

United States Bureau of the Census. *Statistical Abstract of the United States.* Washington, DC: Government Printing Office, annual.

COUNTRY DATA

ABI/Inform. Ann Arbor, MI: University Microfilms International. [Online database and CD-ROM.] Weekly [online], monthly [CD-ROM].

Business Periodicals Index. New York: The H.W. Wilson Company, monthly.

Directory of United States Importers. New York: Journal of Commerce, biennial.

International Financial Statistics Yearbook. Washington, DC: International Monetary Fund, annual.

Overseas Business Reports. Washington, DC: Industry and Trade Administration, monthly.

Predicasts Indexes. Cleveland, OH: Predicasts, biweekly.

5

Questionnaire Design and Development

N*ext question: I believe that life is a constant striving for balance, requiring frequent tradeoffs between morality and necessity, within a cyclic pattern of joy and sadness, forging a trail of bittersweet memories until one slips, inevitably, into the jaws of death. Agree or disagree?*

—Caption of drawing by Geo. Price;
© 1989 The New Yorker Magazine, Inc.
Reprinted by permission.

The term *survey research* describes studies designed to collect observations about social phenomena systematically through interviews and questionnaires administered to individual samples of a population. Survey results are widely used by academic institutions, businesses, and government agencies; they have come to play an important role in journalism and legal proceedings as well. Estimates derived from "surveys of surveys" indicate that at least 100 million survey interviews were conducted between 1971 and 1976 in the United States, and more than 28 million interviews were performed by telephone in 1980 (Turner and Martin 1984, p. 30).

A vast literature exists on the complex subject of questionnaire design; however, this chapter can only skim the guidance, ideas, and examples available there. Accordingly, throughout the ensuing paragraphs, references to additional source materials will be cited.

Note: This chapter was prepared by Professor Alvin J. Silk, Harvard Business School.

A Multistage Development Process

After defining the purpose of your study and deciding—perhaps tentatively—what data collection method you will employ, you will be ready to begin. As new issues arise, of course, you may find it necessary to refine and modify your goals and approaches. The following outline shows the steps involved in developing the questionnaire. These steps, similar to those proposed by Sheatsley (1983) and Sudman and Bradburn (1982), are explained in more detail beginning on page 59.

1. **Decide What Information Should Be Sought**
    a. Determine what data you need to address your research purposes and questions.
    b. Translate data needs into respondent/informant tasks.

2. **Draft Questions**
    a. Consult sources for design guidelines.
    b. Choose question type.
    c. Write questions and check for wording problems.
    d. Design response format.
    e. Determine requirements for classification information, e.g., respondent's demographic characteristics and formulate questions for same.

3. **Design Questionnaire**
    a. Draft introduction and instructions.
    b. Arrange sequence of questions.
    c. Format questionnaire and code for processing.

4. **Review First Draft Critically and Revise**
    a. Identify omissions and excesses.
    b. Administer to a naive (unaware) subject, solicit feedback, and estimate completion time required.
    c. Apply question critique checklist.

5. **Pilot Test, Repeat Step #4, and Revise**

Survey Errors: Problems and Opportunities

Measurement of any quantity is, of course, subject to error, which is defined as the difference between observation and true value; estimates obtained from surveys are no exception. The quality of survey results reflects how the survey was designed and executed and the findings analyzed. It is important to recognize the possible sources of error in survey

Exhibit 5-1

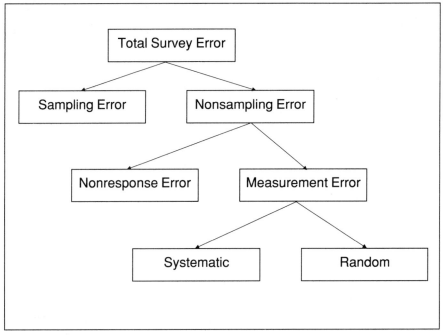

results. *Exhibit 5-1* outlines the major types of errors encountered in surveys.

Sampling Error

The first distinction to be made is between sampling and non-sampling errors (Cochran 1977). Sampling errors arise because observations are obtained from a sample rather than from a complete population. If the measurement process were to be repeated again and again, each time drawing from a different sample of the same size, the results would exhibit some random variation from sample to sample. Thus, the news media announce that "a nationwide poll of 1,000 adults found that 63% favor passage of the Equal Rights Amendment, with a margin of error of plus or minus 3 percentage points." The "margin of error" noted in such reports, typically 3 percentage points, ordinarily refers to estimates of sampling error.

Nonsampling Error

Ignoring nonsampling error results in understatements of total survey error. Converse and Traugott (1986) reviewed data derived from comparisons of similar or matched surveys of the same public policy issues. Analysis of the comparisons indicated that the discrepancies exceeded those expected to arise from random sampling errors, leading them to suggest that "the conventional 3 percentage point warning is rarely a conservative one" (p. 1095).

Nonsampling errors may be divided into: (a) *nonresponse errors,* which occur when responses from certain members of the original sample are not obtained, and (b) *measurement errors,* sometimes called "response effects" (Sudman and Bradburn 1974, pp. 2-4), which can be traced to the instruments used (i.e., interviewers or questionnaires) or to the participants.

Findings from a study conducted for AT&T illustrate these distinctions (Assael and Keon 1982). A questionnaire mailed to a sample of small businesses (defined as firms having three phone lines or fewer) included the following item: "What was the company's average telephone bill over the last three months?" Of the original sample, 58% returned the questionnaire and responded to the above item. The mean bill reported was $136/firm/month. Using billing records, AT&T was able to determine the actual telephone bills for both the total sample to which the questionnaire had been sent as well as the 58% that responded. These "true" (mean) values were found to be $113 for the total original sample and $127 for the sample of responding firms.

That the actual monthly bills of responding firms on average exceeded those of the total original sample by $14/firm ($127-$113) indicates that *nonresponse* operated to yield a biased sample of responding firms, wherein heavy telephone users were overrepresented and lighter users were underrepresented. Comparing the reported and actual bills of responding firms, we further see that *systematic measurement error* was present, leading to overreporting by an average of $9/firm ($136-$127). Consider the consequences of relying on the billings reported by survey respondents to estimate the total sample's true bill. The combined effects of sample bias due to nonresponse and overreporting due to positive measurement errors would have led to an estimate of mean bill size inflated by $23/firm ($136-$113), or about 20%.

Of course, it is unusual to have access to the "true" values of quantities estimated in surveys, but comparisons like those discussed above serve as a sobering reminder of the challenge inherent in designing a survey. What can be done to minimize fallibility? Familiarity with the nature and sources of survey errors can help you ask the right questions. For example, in the above case, could nonresponse bias have been reduced by using a different method of data collection, such as face-to-face or telephone interviews?[1] In a small business, who is likely to be most knowledgeable about the firm's telephone expenses and thus best qualified to serve as a survey informant? Would measurement error be diminished if the questionnaire encouraged the informant to consult records? Would it be preferable to request information about telephone expenses in each of three specified months rather than ask for an "average for the past three months"? An understanding of possible errors will expand your range of options and often lead to methods that improve accuracy.

Nonresponse Error

Nonresponse error reduces the size of the sample available for analysis, constituting a threat to the final sample's representativeness. Because sampling error varies inversely with sample size, any such reduction in sample size will increase the magnitude of random sampling error if no allowance for nonresponse is made when planning the study.

More seriously, nonresponse is likely to cause systematic error or bias, as was the case in the telephone expense study discussed earlier. Although the essence of a probability sample is the specification of procedures to ensure that respondents/informants are randomly drawn, selectivity invariably arises once particular data collection methods are introduced. If respondents are themselves a random subsample of the total sample originally drawn, then nonresponse would not bias the final results. However, because responding to an interview or questionnaire is a conscious social act, it is unlikely to conform to the impartial laws of probability. Hence, it is imperative to minimize both the nonresponse rate and opportunities for uncontrolled selectivity to influence participation in a study.

Controlling Access. Clearly, availability and motivation determine who responds to surveys and who does not. There are two ways to exert some control over availability or access. The first is choice of data collection method. The options are personal interviews (face-to-face or telephone) and self-administered questionnaires (delivered and retrieved via mail or personally). The magnitude of error will vary, depending on the survey's subject matter and the population studied. No one method dominates the others for all purposes and occasions, and the choice involves trade-offs. For example, in a study of single-parent households, telephone interviews may produce a higher response rate than a mail questionnaire, but if the subject matter is socially sensitive (e.g., controversial or threatening), then the mail questionnaire may offer respon-

---

1.   Assael and Keon (1982) tested these alternatives and found that both face-to-face and telephone interviews led to larger nonresponse biases than did the mail questionnaire.

dents greater assurance of anonymity, thereby diminishing selectivity bias. Dillman (1978, chapter 2) presents a useful comparison of personal and telephone interviews and mail questionnaires.

A second means of controlling access concerns administering the chosen data collection method: deciding when to schedule fieldwork and whether to provide advanced notification and reminders or callbacks to sample members. Following such procedures can enhance response rates. Reviews of relevant literature and data can be found in Steeh (1981) for personal interviews, Wiseman and McDonald (1979) for telephone surveys, and Fox, Crask, and Kim (1988) for mail surveys. Valuable information on scheduling face-to-face and telephone interviews is presented in Weeks et al. (1980, 1987).

Motivating Response. A request to give an interview or to fill out a questionnaire represents an intrusion. Why would or should an individual agree to participate and exert the effort to respond to questions conscientiously?

Dillman (1978, pp. 12-19) offers a perceptive analysis of respondent behavior as a special case of "social exchange": An individual's propensity to engage in a particular behavior is a function of the expected rewards and costs that person associates with doing so. Dillman suggests three steps that can maximize survey response: *"minimize* the *costs* of responding, *maximize* the *rewards* for doing so, and *establish trust* that those rewards will be delivered" (p. 12, emphasis added). Dillman's suggestions for accomplishing these steps bear repeating:

1. Reward respondents by:
   a. making them feel special,
   b. expressing appreciation verbally,
   c. using a consulting approach (explain that you're seeking "advice"),
   d. supporting their expressed values,
   e. offering tangible rewards,
   f. ensuring that the questionnaire is interesting.
2. Reduce costs to the respondents by:
   a. making the task appear brief,
   b. striving for brevity and clarity to alleviate the physical and mental effort required,
   c. taking care not to offend or embarrass,
   d. taking care not to patronize,
   e. eliminating any direct monetary costs (e.g., postage or telephone charges).
3. Establish trust by:
   a. providing a token of appreciation in advance,

b. identifying with a reputable organization,

c. identifying with other exchange (similar) relationships.

Measurement Error

Thus far, we have focused on mean levels, computed by aggregating and averaging across the relevant data for each sample member. Thus, in the telephone example, on average, small businesses overstated their monthly telephone bills by $14 when responding to a mail survey. We would, of course, expect some variability among individual firms in not only the magnitude of their reporting errors, but also their direction—most overreporting, but some underreporting, and perhaps a few being perfectly accurate. Hence, we need to recognize the possible presence of both systematic and random error components in responses to a measuring instrument.

The distinction between systematic and random measurement errors is closely related to reliability and validity. *Reliability* is concerned with random measurement error: how stable, consistent, or reproducible are the responses obtained from some measurement instrument. *Validity* is concerned with both systematic and random measurement error: whether an instrument or procedure measures the concept that it claims to measure and, if so, how adequately. What do SAT scores or GMAT scores or Nielsen television program ratings really measure? Do advertising copy tests measure advertising effectiveness? What are meaningful indicators of corporate excellence and innovativeness? The presence of both systematic and random measurement errors in responses threatens a measure's validity. Therefore, in evaluating a measure or choosing among procedures it is important to consider their comparative reliability and validity. A discussion of methods for assessing reliability and validity may be found in Bohrnstedt (1983).

What Data Should Be Sought?

The first step in developing a questionnaire is deciding what information you want to gather. The challenge is to assume the role of an interpreter who must not only speak the "language" of both study sponsor and respondent but also understand their points of view. To accomplish this "translation," you must first map your research purposes and goals and transform them into data requirements, then define the role and tasks to be performed by survey participants in supplying those data, and finally formulate questions that will elicit the target reports and assessments.

Types of Roles and Data

The first step is to generate a list of the kinds of data needed to address the research questions or hypotheses motivating your study. It is helpful to classify the items in the list according to the matrix shown in *Exhibit 5-2*, which cross-classifies three types of data with two kinds of roles that a participant may be asked to assume in providing those data.

When a question asks a participant to say something about herself or himself, that person is cast in the role of a *respondent*. Alternatively, questions may ask about other persons or social entities, such as one or more members of the participant's family, group, organization, or community; that participant then serves as an *informant* (Seidler 1974). We use the term *reports* to denote responses that pertain to *behavior* (i.e., past or current acts, events, and practices); we apply the label *assessments* to responses that relate to mental states: either *cognitions* (i.e., information, knowledge, beliefs, judgments, images, and perceptions) or *affects* (i.e., feelings, emotions, and satisfactions).

These distinctions between types of roles and data are important because they begin to clarify the nature of the study participant's task. For example, reporting on one's own behavior is quite different from serving as an informant on an organization's practices. Accordingly, the nature and magnitude of the errors that occur in response to these two types of questions are likely to be different.

Exhibit 5-2

Role of Participant	Type of Data		
	Behavioral Reports	**Cognitive Assessments**	**Affective Assessments**
Respondent	Actions	Knowledge	Preferences
	Events	Opinions/Beliefs	Attitudes
Informant	Practices	Perceptions	Satisfactions
		Judgments	

Task Considerations

To conduct a successful survey, you must satisfy three conditions for each respondent/informant: (a) comprehension of his or her role and the information you seek, (b) accessibility to that information, and (c) motivation to assume the role and engage in the requested task behavior (Cannell and Kahn 1968). The ease or difficulty of meeting these conditions varies with the task. Based on an extensive review of research on measurement errors in surveys, Sudman and Bradburn (1974, pp. 8-13) formulated the following hypotheses about how various dimensions of the respondent's task contribute to error level in their responses:

1. The greater the *degree of structure,* the lower the magnitude of measurement errors.
2. The greater the *problems of self-presentation* elicited by a question (i.e., the less socially desirable some responses are perceived to be), the greater the pressure on the respondent to answer a question, or, the more controversial the subject matter, the greater the magnitude of measurement errors.
3. The greater the *saliency* of the information sought, the lower the magnitude of measurement errors.

The problems of low saliency and self-presentation will vary according to the topic under study and the population surveyed; what can be done to ameliorate their effects may be limited. For some of these problems, however, there are special procedures that may be useful. For example, Sudman and Bradburn (1974, pp. 9 and 68-84) point out that low saliency is an issue primarily because of memory errors, which may be reduced by employing procedures that aid or limit recall, such as by providing specific cues (e.g., lists, pictures, and dates) and encouraging subjects to consult records. Similarly, there are special methods of asking survey questions on controversial or socially sensitive topics (Bradburn and Sudman 1979), such as the "randomized response technique," which preserves the confidentiality of individual responses (Fox and Tracy 1986). Indirect and unobtrusive methods of measuring attitudes may also be considered (Kidder and Campbell 1970; Webb et al. 1981).

Another challenge in structuring the participant's task is deciding whether to ask a global (summary) question or a series of specific questions that break the overall task into component parts. This issue frequently arises in connection with the use of informants who are asked, as Seidler (1974, p. 817) has wryly noted, "at least implicitly, to perform calculations otherwise left to the computer." Specific questions are especially helpful when they assess such properties as the price and quality of one firm's products compared with competitors' (Phillips, Chang, and Buzzell 1983), patterns of influence in organizational decision making

(Silk and Kalwani 1982), and control in customer-supplier relations (Phillips 1981).

When one uses general questions, giving respondents detailed instructions about what data or judgments are relevant and how to make calculations simplifies the task and reduces the possibility of measurement error.

The questionnaire designer needs to be diligent in monitoring these matters and to heed the warning of Cannell, Oksenberg, and Converse (1977, p. 309): "The demands placed on the respondents by many survey questions are greater than generally has been realized, and the respondents' inability or unwillingness to meet these demands is a major source of invalidity."

Questionnaire Design

Sources of Design Guidelines and Advice

In designing a question, three basic issues must be addressed: (1) what form of question should be employed, (2) how it should be worded, and (3) whether response alternatives should be presented, and, if so, which ones and in what format. A variety of solutions are available for each of these design problems, but you should choose carefully because survey results can be influenced by the form and wording of questions and response categories. Therefore, be familiar with the options available and guidelines for choosing among them.

A considerable literature on questionnaire design is available. The following are some reference works for the novice questionnaire designer:

- J. Converse and S. Presser, *Survey Questions: Handcrafting the Standardized Questionnaire.* Beverly Hills, Cal.: Sage, 1986. (paperback).
- D. Dillman, *Mail and Telephone Surveys.* New York: Wiley, 1978.
- S. Payne, *The Art of Asking Questions.* Princeton: Princeton University Press, 1951.
- S. Sudman and N. Bradburn, *Asking Questions: A Practical Guide to Questionnaire Design.* San Francisco: Jossey-Bass, 1982.

The prescriptions offered in these works are based on a modest amount of scientific evidence combined with large amounts of experience and common sense. Converse and Presser provide the most compact treatment (75 pages and available in paperback), but their text does not deal explicitly with self-administered questionnaires. Dillman treats both mail and telephone surveys in a comprehensive and detailed manner and includes a useful framework for choosing among face-to-face, telephone, and mail questionnaires. Payne's is the classic work on questionnaire wording, a storehouse of examples and thoughtful counsel that is also enjoyable to read. Sudman and Bradburn offer balanced and comprehensive coverage of all three methods of data collection. Other relevant reviews are found in Dijkstra and van der Zouwen (1982) and Hippler et al. (1987).

The impact of small changes in question wording has often been demonstrated in simple experiments known as "split ballot" studies, in which different versions of a question are administered to randomly selected halves of the same sample. Evidence from such studies can help in identifying sources of measurement errors and in suggesting ways to avoid or reduce them. Consider the following example from a routine consumer survey carried out for a chemical firm.

Respondents in a nationwide probability sample of 1,000 adults were asked to agree or disagree with a series of opinion statements about wash-and-wear clothing (O'Neill 1967). The sample was randomly split; one half was presented with a "positively" worded version of an item, and the other half, a "negatively" worded counterpart. *Exhibit 5-3* shows

Exhibit 5-3

Item	Wording*	Response (%)			
		Favor.	Unfav.	Neut.	Total
1. Clothes like these (cut/increase) the cost of keeping clothes clean.	Pos.	79	12	9	100
	Neg.	76	13	11	100
	Diff.	+3			
2. Clothes like these are (easy/hard) to get dirt out with washing.	Pos.	88	6	6	100
	Neg.	76	12	12	100
	Diff.	+12			

Source: Data reported in O'Neill (1967, pp. 99-100).

* The alternative wordings used in the two versions of each question are shown in parentheses—the first word represents the "positive" wording, and the second the "negative" wording. Note that "disagreeing" with a "negatively" worded statement is treated as a "favorable" response.

the distributions of responses observed for two of the questions—shown as percentages of each split sample (n=500), which expressed a favorable, unfavorable, or neutral opinion about wash-and-wear clothing.

Note that for both items, favorable opinions were more likely to be expressed for positively worded versions of the statements than for the negatively worded alternative. The standard error of the difference between estimates (of a proportion for two samples), each consisting of 500 respondents, is about 3%. Thus, the difference of 3 percentage points in Item #1 is within the range of differences to be expected due to random sampling error. However, the difference of 12 percentage points in Item #2 is much larger than that which can be confidently attributed to sampling fluctuations. It is an example of the type of measurement error or response effect that results from unbalanced questions—questions that present only one side of an issue or opinion (Schuman and Presser 1981, chapter 7).

In light of such findings, generally accepted survey practice favors balanced questions (e.g., Payne 1951, chapter 4). In some instances, balance may be achieved in a straightforward manner—for example, "Do you support or oppose passage of the Equal Rights Amendment?" Phrasing the question about wash-and-wear clothing in this manner would be more difficult, however. A construction such as, "Do wash-and-wear clothes increase or decrease cleaning costs?" poses another difficulty, that of an "implied alternative" (Payne 1951, p. 56). A better formulation would be: "Compared with wool, do wash-and-wear clothes increase or decrease cleaning costs?"

In addition to applying the kinds of general guidelines and advice found in the recommended references and illustrated above, you should also seek out expertise bearing on the topic under investigation. Informal interviews or focus groups with a small number of respondents from the target population are very useful. They can help compensate for whatever social distance may exist between the questionnaire designer and interviewer and his or her informants or respondents, thereby revealing any problems of unfamiliar language and concepts, low salience, or threatening subject matter. In many fields, there are specialized measurement instruments with tested reliability or validity. You can find such material through a literature search or discussions with people who have conducted studies in the same area. You can also learn much from examining a questionnaire that has already been used in similar work.

Questionnaire Organization

The next task is to arrange the sequence of questions to form the questionnaire. Dillman (1978, pp. 123-127) suggests four principles for deciding how questions should be ordered.

1. Order questions along a descending gradient of social usefulness or importance; those that the respondent/informant is most likely to see as useful come first and those least useful come last.
2. Group questions that are similar in content together—and within content areas, by type of question (e.g., reports of behavior versus assessments of attitudes).
3. Take advantage of connections that subjects are likely to make among groups of questions to create a sense of flow and continuity.
4. Within any topic area, position questions that are least likely to be objectionable before the more objectionable ones.

Applying these principles often involves making judgments and compromises that should be reexamined after pretesting. Questions used to obtain information on demographic characteristics and other background or classification variables are usually placed at the end. In designing such questions, keep in mind anticipated comparisons of the study's results with other studies or sources of information. For surveys among the general population, there are certain standard demographic categories (e.g., age, education, income), which are presented in Sudman and Bradburn (1982, chapter 7).

Two other tasks must be done. First, prepare cover letters, introductions, and instructions. Dillman's (1978, chapters 5 and 7) discussion of these topics is very useful. It is important to address growing public and government concern over privacy and confidentiality issues in relation to the collection and uses of survey data (National Research Council 1979). Promises of confidentiality made to respondents and informants are a responsibility that the researcher must take very seriously. Second, format the questionnaire and precode it to facilitate data processing. Dillman (1978) and Sudman and Bradburn (1982) provide detailed instructions on these matters.

Critical Reviews and Pretests

Critical review and pretesting of the questionnaire are vital. More than one round may be necessary to refine it sufficiently to warrant asking respondents for a serious time commitment. As Sudman and Bradburn (1982, p. 283) advise, "If you do not have the resources to pilot test your questionnaire, don't do the study."

Reviews and tests should help identify excesses and omissions. Virtually all discussions of questionnaire development admonish the designer to ask, "Is this question really necessary or merely interesting?" and urge, "Keep it short and simple." One useful exercise is to go through a draft of the questionnaire item by item and simulate the outcome by creating dummy tables indicating how the data will eventually be analyzed and reported. Such a disciplined effort invariably pays off by uncovering both excesses and omissions.

A tedious but nonetheless effective way to detect wording problems is to check each questionnaire item against the following list of questions proposed by Dillman (1978, pp. 97-118):

1. Will the words be uniformly understood?
2. Does the question contain obscure abbreviations or unconventional phrases?
3. Is the question too vague?
4. Is the question too precise?
5. Is the question biased?
6. Is the question objectionable?
7. Is the question too demanding?
8. Is it a double question?
9. Does the question have a double negative?
10. Are the answers mutually exclusive?
11. Does the question assume too much about what respondents know?
12. Is the question technically accurate?
13. Is an appropriate time referent provided?
14. Can the question be understood when taken out of order or context?
15. Can responses be compared to existing information?

Summary

Questionnaire designers should think of response behavior as a special form of social exchange. The challenge is to construct a questionnaire that promotes access, comprehension, and motivation among participants. It must contain carefully defined and structured roles and tasks with the goals of establishing trust, minimizing costs, and maximizing rewards resulting from participation. Much can be done to reduce nonsampling errors and enhance the ultimate value of a survey by following an orderly, sequential approach to the development of measuring instruments. Such a process should make explicit provisions for obtaining early feedback through pretesting and checking the instrument for consistency with relevant design guidelines.

References

Assael, H., and J. Keon. (1982). "Nonsampling vs. Sampling Errors in Survey Research." *Journal of Marketing* 46 (Spring): 114-123.

Bohrnstedt, G. (1983). "Measurement." Chapter 3 in P. Rossi, J. Wright, and A. Anderson, eds. *Handbook of Survey Research*. New York: Academic Press, 70-121.

Bradburn, N., and S. Sudman. (1979). *Improving Interview Method and Questionnaire Design*. San Francisco: Jossey-Bass.

Cannell, C., and R. Kahn. (1968). "Interviewing." Chapter 15 in G. Lindzey and E. Aronson, eds. *Handbook of Social Psychology*. 2nd ed. Vol. 2. Reading, Mass.: Addison-Wesley, 526-595.

Cannell, C., L. Oksenberg, and J. Converse. (1977). "Striving for Response Accuracy: Experiments in New Interviewing Techniques." *Journal of Marketing Research* 14 (August): 306-315.

Cochran, W. (1977). *Sampling Techniques*. 3rd ed. New York: Wiley.

Converse, J., and M. Traugott. (1986). "Assessing the Accuracy of Polls and Surveys." *Science* 234 (November 28): 1094-1098.

Converse, J., and S. Presser. (1986). *Survey Questions: Handcrafting the Standardized Questionnaire*. Beverly Hills, Cal.: Sage.

Dijkstra, W., and J. van der Zouwen, eds. (1982). *Response Behavior in the Survey Interview*. New York: Academic Press.

Dillman, D. (1978). *Mail and Telephone Surveys*. New York: Wiley.

Fox, J., and P. Tracy. (1986). *Randomized Response: A Method for Sensitive Surveys*. Beverly Hills, Cal.: Sage Publications.

Fox, R., M. Crask, and J. Kim. (1988). "Mail Survey Response Rate." *Public Opinion Quarterly* 52 (Winter): 467-491.

Hippler, H., N. Schwartz, and S. Sudman, eds. (1987). *Social Information Processing and Survey Methodology*. New York: Springer-Verlag.

Kalwani, M., and A. Silk. (1982). "On the Reliability and Predictive Validity of Purchase Intention Measures." *Marketing Science* 1 (Summer): 243-286.

Kidder, L., and D. Campbell. (1970). "The Indirect Testing of Social Attitudes." Chapter 20 in G. Summers, ed. *Attitude Measurement*. Chicago: Rand-McNally, 333-385.

National Research Council. (1979). *Privacy and Confidentiality as Factors in Survey Response*. Washington, DC: National Academy of Sciences.

O'Neill, H. (1967). "Response Style Influences in Public Opinion Surveys." *Public Opinion Quarterly* 31 (Spring): 95-102.

Payne, S. (1951). *The Art of Asking Questions*. Princeton: Princeton University Press.

Phillips, L. (1981). "Assessing Measurement Error in Key Informant Reports: A Methodological Note on Organizational Analysis in Marketing." *Journal of Marketing Research* 18 (November): 395-415.

Phillips, L., D. Chang, and R. Buzzell. (1983). "Product Quality, Cost Position, and Business Performance: A Test of Some Key Hypotheses." *Journal of Marketing* 47 (Spring): 26-43.

Schuman, H., and S. Presser. (1981). *Questions and Answers in Attitude Surveys*. New York: Academic Press.

Seidler, J. (1974). "On Using Informants: A Technique for Collecting Quantitative Data and Controlling Measurement Error in Organization Analysis." *American Sociological Review*. (December): 816-831.

Sheatsley, P. (1983). "Questionnaire Construction and Item Writing." Chapter 6 in P. Rossi, J. Wright, and A. Anderson, eds. *Handbook of Survey Research*. New York: Academic Press, 195-230.

Silk, A., and M. Kalwani. (1982). "Measuring Influence in Organizational Purchase Decisions." *Journal of Marketing Research* 19 (May): 165-181.

Steeh, C. (1981). "Trends in Nonresponse Rates, 1952-1979." *Public Opinion Quarterly*. 45 (Spring): 40-57.

Sudman, S., and N. Bradburn. (1974). *Response Effects in Surveys*. Chicago: Aldine.

Sudman, S., and N. Bradburn. (1982). *Asking Questions: A Practical Guide to Questionnaire Design*. San Francisco: Jossey-Bass.

Turner, C., and E. Martin, eds. (1984). *Surveying Subjective Phenomena*. Vol. I. New York: Russell Sage Foundation.

Webb, E., D. Campbell, R. Schwartz, L. Sechrest, and J. Grove. (1981). *Nonreactive Measures in the Social Sciences*. 2nd ed. Boston: Houghton Mifflin.

Weeks, M., B. Jones, R. Folsom, Jr., and C. Bernard. (1980). "Optimal Times to Contact Sample Households." *Public Opinion Quarterly* 44 (Spring): 101-114.

Weeks, M., R. Kulka, and S. Pierson. (1987). "Optimal Scheduling for a Telephone Survey." *Public Opinion Quarterly* 51 (Winter): 540-549.

Wiseman, F., and P. McDonald. (1979). "Noncontact and Refusal Rates in Consumer Telephone Surveys." *Journal of Marketing Research* 16 (November): 478-484.

6

Supervising Field Studies Projects: A Faculty Guide

F ield studies projects can—and usually do—provide a valuable learning experience for students. Much of the value comes from their relationship with you, the faculty supervisor.

The faculty supervisor-student team relationship depends on the nature of the project and what supervisors and students want from each other and from doing the project. Accordingly, this discussion will suggest areas for consideration as you begin working with your project teams.

As faculty supervisor, you play three roles: counselor, teacher, and judge. You are not a project leader or client liaison. If you have generated the project, however, you do have responsibility for taking action if you perceive lack of client commitment to the project or if the project is veering off track.

Moreover, if the project is expected to contribute to your research and/or course development, you may play a more active part in its design and execution. At the same time, it is important that you do not preempt student initiative and responsibility for the conduct and outcome of the project.

In early meetings with student team members, it is essential that you make your expectations clear. On what matters do you wish to be kept informed? What kinds of issues should be on your meeting agendas? Will you be available on an as-needed basis or do you wish to meet regularly with the student team? How do you want your students to prepare for your meetings with them? What progress reports (e.g., memoranda,

Note: This chapter was prepared by Professor E. Raymond Corey, Harvard Business School.

project definition statements, report drafts) would you like to have, and when? You should make clear as early as possible any professional interest you may have in their topic as a possible case subject, or for research, or for your learning generally; the project can be designed to take your interests into account.

Early conversations with the project team should leave room, as well, for some discussion of their expectations of you and for their questions about how you like to work as a faculty supervisor. Any ambiguities or differences in expectations detract from the benefits and enjoyment of the field studies experience. At the very least, if the terms of a constructive relationship are not worked out early, there are likely to be unnecessary delays in getting started on the project and frustration on both sides.

Counseling

Although it is difficult to anticipate what issues may emerge as you counsel your project team, there are three topics that will be part of any field studies agenda: (1) problem definition, (2) client relationships, and (3) schedule.

Problem Definition. For both faculty-generated and student-initiated projects, the preliminary statement of the topic or the issues to be studied will almost always be refined as the team becomes involved in the project. The faculty supervisor can help by urging team members to create with the client a mission statement that responds to client needs, meets your academic standards, provides a worthwhile learning experience, and can be done in the time available.

Client Relations. Students may have difficulty obtaining the cooperation of key client managers. Some managers may resist the idea of a study; some may be unavailable; and confidentiality concerns may deter others from providing necessary data.

Another common problem is gaining access to, and securing the cooperation of, managers who have the authority to "open the right doors—and files" and implement the team's recommendations. It is also important to ensure that students have access to managers who can help students learn about a particular field, an industry, or a company.

Gaining access to client personnel and data is an important challenge for students doing a field project. Some intervention by the faculty supervisor may be needed, however, if students cannot gain access to sources of information by themselves. If you have generated the project, it may be appropriate for you to speak directly about access problems with your original contact person.

Schedule. Most students have never done a large-scale field study, so they may be unsure about how to allocate their time or may not appreciate the importance of setting interim deadlines. Requiring them to make a project schedule for discussion with you early in the study will help avoid problems later. Ideally, the schedule should be "front-end loaded" for project planning and team building and "back-end loaded" for report preparation.

A note of caution on schedules: students' meetings with the client and other field visits should be planned around their class schedules. Missing classes to pursue field projects should not be permissible. For this reason, as well, the final oral presentation should be scheduled on campus. If the final meeting of key client managers must be held at a company location, it should not conflict with class attendance.

Teaching

Students can learn a great deal from their faculty supervisor during a field study. The project becomes a tutorial that encompasses conception, data gathering, analysis, and recommendations. It is important for you to contribute as much as possible to your students from your own knowledge of how to do field research.

Your tutorial may address a variety of subjects: developing a project structure, choosing research methods, interviewing, dealing with client politics, managing relationships within the team, writing reports, and making graphic presentations. As the team's counselor, you can identify other faculty who can contribute expertise as needed and direct attention to other sources of information. Most important, your support and availability will help ensure that the project is successful and that students learn as much as possible.

Judging

Evaluating field studies projects and assigning grades to team members pose special challenges. First, each project is unique. Second, most faculty supervisors have only one or two projects to grade and do not have the benefit of performance comparisons across a large number of projects. Third, because these are team efforts, it may be difficult to assess the quality of each individual student's work.

Grading Elements. A reasonable approach to evaluation is to break down project performance into those elements that all field projects have in common and to assess them for the project as a whole. Unlike an exam, a field studies project can be evaluated according to both process and product. The quality of the process is reflected in part by the team members' relationships with each other, with the client, and with the faculty supervisor. Data gathering and analysis are also process elements. In terms of product, the project proposal and the written and oral reports may be assessed for their usefulness and overall quality, using a range of criteria. *Exhibit 6-1* offers suggestions for developing an evaluation form that can serve at the outset as a contract between you and the students and ultimately as an evaluation form.

In choosing evaluation criteria, it is useful to understand how performance measures can affect process and working relationships. Some faculty members, for example, do not evaluate team-supervisor relationships, thinking that to do so would lead to a more structured and guarded give-and-take. Some have elected to give all team members the same grade, believing that to differentiate would foster competition rather than collaboration. Clearly, the faculty supervisor must decide what aspects of performance to evaluate and what evidence to use. But however grading and giving feedback are done, they are important to the learning process and must be done with care.

Grading Inputs. For the most part, the evaluation of the project and of individual team members will come out of your work with the team and your own assessment of the written and oral reports. It may be useful, however, to involve both the students and the client managers in the grading process. You may ask client managers to give you their perceptions of how the students related to people in their organization and of the usefulness of the final reports. Students may be asked to evaluate each other's contribution using the form in *Exhibit 6-2.* Instructors who have used student evaluations in the grading process have found these helpful in identifying "outliers," i.e., those who are recognized by their teammates as making especially strong contributions or those who contributed much less than others to the success of the project.

Performance Feedback. As for final grades, the practice for some faculty supervisors has been to give the same grade to each student—a grade that represents the supervisor's evaluation of the project as a whole. Other supervisors, using student inputs and their own assessments of the contributions of each student and the project as a whole, have assigned individual grades. The former grading practice tends to reward team effort; the latter recognizes individual student performance. To achieve both purposes, each team member may be given two grades: one based on your evaluation of the project and one that reflects his or her individual performance. In most cases, each grade will be the same, with exceptional performance—either well above or below average—reflected by a difference in the second of the two grades.

In addition to receiving grades, your students will also benefit from your assessing their performance in the different phases of their project. A suggested evaluation form is shown in *Exhibit 6-3;* it provides feedback on each element of the project as delineated in the original "contract" (*Exhibit 6-1*). Probably the most useful feedback that you can give would be a qualitative commentary. *Exhibit 6-4* gives an example; it is a memorandum written by a faculty member to student team members (the names have been disguised).

Exhibit 6-1

FIELD STUDIES TEAM MEMBER EVALUATIONS

PROJECT:_____

_____% **Project Proposal**

Clarity of issue definition

Identification of data sources

Completeness and feasibility of action plan, including
- travel and interview schedule
- team meeting schedule
- progress checkpoints ·

Completeness and feasibility of project budget

Quality of proposal in communicating with the client

_____% **Client Relationships**

Quality of interactions with client personnel

Ability to listen and to ask useful questions

Effective use of client time

Level of preparedness at meetings with client personnel

Ability to meet deadlines

Prompt notification and discussion of possible changes in project
scope

Willingness and ability to understand the client company

_____% **Team Member and Supervisor Relationships**

Ability of team members to work together effectively

Effectiveness in setting and holding to meeting schedules

Effectiveness in organizing the project and structuring team
members' assignments

Commitment to the project

Good use of supervisor's time, including
- setting meaningful meeting agenda
- being prepared
- keeping supervisor informed

1

Exhibit 6-1 continued

FIELD STUDIES EVALUATION cont'd

_____% **Data Gathering and Analysis**

Competence in selecting, designing, and using research instruments, e.g., questionnaires, focus group interviews, one-on-
 one interviews

Interviewing effectiveness as demonstrated by the amount and quality of data gathered

Resourcefulness in identifying and obtaining relevant internal client
 data

Resourcefulness in finding and using outside data sources and relevant past research

Creativity in developing hypotheses for testing as the work proceeds

Ability to recognize and deal with contradictory evidence

Ability to draw useful conclusions from factual data and to formulate
 sound recommendations supported by sound analysis

_____% **The Written Report**

Completeness and quality of relevant factual information

Soundness of analysis

Creativity, decisiveness, and usefulness of the recommendations

Creativity and realism in the plan of implementation

Clarity and written quality of the final report

_____% **The Oral Presentation**

Quality of the final oral presentation, including
 · focus on essential points of fact and recommendations
 · clarity and persuasiveness of delivery
 · quality of graphic materials
 · effectiveness in conducting an open discussion
 · considerate and informative treatment of questions
Soundness and creativity of the recommendations

2

Exhibit 6-2

Field Studies Team Member Evaluations

PROJECT:_____

Below, please write the name of each student in your team, *EXCLUDING YOURSELF,* and provide your assessment of each colleague's contributions to the effectiveness of the project. Make sure all your percentage figures add to 100%. This information will be kept strictly confidential but will be used by your faculty adviser in the grading process. Thanks for your help.

Name of Student	% of Contribution

100%

Please return this form to your faculty adviser.

Exhibit 6-3

Field Studies Project Evaluation Form

PROJECT:_____

	I	II	III	IV
1. Project proposal				
2. Client relationships				
3. Team member and supervisor relationships				
4. Data gathering and analysis				
5. The written report				
6. The oral report				

Exhibit 6-4

MEMORANDUM

TO: John Doe, Bob Smith, Jane Murphy, Joe Jones
FROM: Professor Sue Brown
SUBJECT: Final Evaluation of ABC Field Study
DATE: May 19

This brief note is my final evaluation of your performance of the ABC Field Study. I had an opportunity for an oral debriefing with John Doe and Bob Smith after the second presentation to ABC, but would like to make sure that the entire team gets the same message.

As we discussed at the beginning of the project, I consider both product and process criteria in assigning grades for the field study project. The attached sheet includes the criteria that I gave you at the beginning of the semester, with my evaluation of how the team did on each of them.

Overall, you did a good job throughout the project, although not a great one. The attachment shows that there were several weaknesses in the "products" (the final presentation and paper) that kept them from Category I status.

First, the team missed an opportunity to use library research to support your ideas on positioning and conjoint analysis, or to compare ABC's strategy with that of leading competitors. While you had a bibliography in the report, there was no evidence of analysis based on the readings. Second, you omitted a discussion of your preliminary data collection at ABC, and your review of past research. That analysis could have strengthened the credibility of your own findings.

The creativity you displayed in the analysis of the trade-off data was excellent in places and leads to some very interesting implications for management. That was the highlight of the project.

The team had several problems on the process side, as shown on the attachment. In comparison with eleven other field study and IRR projects that I have supervised in the last four years, the ABC project was well below the standards set by other groups on several dimensions. First, in use of my time, I often felt that the ABC team asked for "too little, too late." I understand that you may have been taking a cue from what your friends were doing on other field study projects as far as involving the faculty supervisor. Second, you had a more difficult time getting the four of you into a room for a meeting than have other teams I have supervised. I'm not sure of all the rea-

Exhibit 6-4 continued

sons, but the result was less than satisfactory team coordination. Third, there were several occasions when individuals failed to follow through on something that I had asked them to do. Examples include not getting my book back for weeks after I needed it and not giving me the data on short lists. These may seem like small details, but the difference between a good job and an outstanding one often involves quality in the detail.

Based on my assessment, I assigned the group two Category I's and six Category II's. I understand and fully accept the team's reluctance to get involved in allocating the two Category I's among you. I decided to give one to John Doe, for his heroic efforts to keep things from falling through the cracks throughout the project. I gave the second one to Bob Smith, based on my assessment of the four of you in the two presentations to ABC. Since everyone got to participate in the presentation, I selected the one who did the best job.

If Jane or Joe have any concerns or questions about the project, my evaluation, or the distribution of the grades, please feel free to call or come by for a visit. Both Bob and John have concerns, feel uncomfortable that I gave them the higher grades, and wish that there were a way for all of you to earn the same grade.

In closing, I'd like to emphasize that I enjoyed working with each of you and think that you have a very positive impact on the thinking of the executives at ABC. You should be proud of your accomplishments. Grades aside, I hope you feel that you learned something about the software business, teamwork, and the positive and negative aspects of working in a consulting environment. Thanks very much for the hard work that you invested in making the project a success.

Attachment

2

Exhibit 6-4 continued

Criteria for Evaluating Field Study Performance

Name: *ABC Field Study*

Date: *May 1990*

PRODUCT: Research Instrument and Final Report

_∿_ Effectiveness/accuracy of the use of theory or empirical data from previous research (quality, not quantity)

_∿_ Resourcefulness in finding/citing relevant past research

_∿_ Ability to synthesize/interpret conflicting findings from past empirical research

_∿_ Creativity in developing "theory" and hypotheses

_✓_ Subtlety and rigor in defining concepts and relationships

_✓_ Quality of the design of the research instrument (questionnaire, interview script, etc.)

_✓/+_ Creativity/insight in analyzing results

_✓_ Subtlety and rigor in using and interpreting empirical evidence

_+_ Attention to detail (completeness, accuracy, spelling, grammar)

_✓/+_ Power and persuasiveness of the "bottom line" from the study

PROCESS

_✓_ Completeness/quality of planning

_✓_ Ability to work without intensive supervision

_∿_ Skillful and cost-effective use of my time

_∿_ Willingness to keep me informed of progress, potential problems on an ongoing (weekly or biweekly) basis

_✓_ Ability to meet deadlines

_✓/∿_ Willingness to work as a cooperative team member (varied by individual)

_∿_ Demonstrated leadership among peers

_✓_ Handling of relationships with outside people and organizations

_✓_ Creativity and initiative in marshalling resources

_∿_ Willingness to make personal sacrifices for the good of the project; e.g., giving 110%, honoring project commitments

+ = Great! (Category I-level effort)
✓ = Good (solid Category II)
∿ = Needs fine tuning (low Category II- does not meet my expectations)

MBA FIELD STUDIES *was composed at the Harvard Business School Publishing Division using WordPerfect 5.1 and Xerox Ventura Publisher Version 2.0 with Professional Extension. The postscript fonts were output on a AGFA Compugraphic 9400 by Graphics Express. The book was printed at John P. Pow, Co., Inc., using Strathmore Grandee Pyrenees White 80 pound Cover, 60 pound Finch Opaque Vellum for the text, and Pantone colors. The paper used in this publication meets the requirements of the American National Standard for Permanence of Paper for Printed Library Materials Z39.49–1984. The book was bound by Pearl Bookbinding Co., Inc.*